Finding Sharon

Matt Birkbeck

A Summerville Book

2937 Rt. 611 #637 Tannersville, PA 18360

Visit the author at www.mattbirkbeck.com.

Library of Congress Cataloging-in-Publication Data

Finding Sharon / Matt Birkbeck

ISBN 978-7324917-1-7

1. Murder – Oklahoma – Case studies. 2. Murder victims – Oklahoma – Case Studies 3. Prison – Florida – Case Studies 4. Criminal Investigation – Florida – Case Studies. I. Title

"And let us not grow weary of doing good, for in due season we will reap, if we do not give up."

GALATIANS 6:9

Prologue

I n 2004 I wrote a book I called *A Beautiful Child*. On the surface, there was nothing really beautiful about it. In fact, it was a horrendous story, one that involved a young woman who worked as a stripper and prostitute and who died in April 1990 following a suspicious hit-and-run accident that was later ruled a homicide.

With the exceptions of a much older husband and two-year-old son, she had no family. And her only friends at the time were the handful of hardened young women who danced with her at a seedy strip club in Tulsa, Oklahoma.

Her death would barely make the obituary page in the local newspaper.

But someone thought it was important to post on the Doe Network website a tidbit that the woman had been kidnapped as a toddler and raised by the same man she called her father and, later, her husband. Even more horrifying, a few years after her death, that man, Franklin Delano Floyd, would kidnap her son from his first-grade class at gunpoint. The boy, Michael, would never be seen again.

So this wasn't an ordinary story, and I wanted to dig deeper.

I would soon learn that the young woman and Floyd had used many aliases as they traveled the country. During her years in high school she was known as Sharon Marshall. After enrolling at Forest Park High School near Atlanta in the 1980s, Sharon impressed everyone with her intellect. She routinely earned As and Bs, was a lieutenant colonel in the Air Force ROTC, and earned a full scholarship to Georgia Tech to study aerospace engineering. She was beautiful and had the smarts to match.

Sharon was a rock star. But what really struck me wasn't her academic record and other great accomplishments or the fact that she was able to succeed at a high level at school despite her disturbing home life, where she had been sexually, physically, and psychologically abused for years. It was her compassion, kindness, inner strength, and tolerance of others—her *humanity*—in the face of such unending horror.

But, of course, Sharon wasn't her real name, and when the book was finished two great mysteries remained: what was her true identity, and what became of her son, Michael?

My hope was that *A Beautiful Child* would provide both answers. But like my first book, *A Deadly Secret*, about the New York real estate scion Robert Durst, it was another complex story that, when published, did not have an ending.

And not that I didn't try.

When I bought into the story of Sharon Marshall I knew I had to devote all my attention and resources to it. At the time, I was working as a correspondent for *People* magazine and had a full-time newspaper job. With *People*, I could accept or turn down an assignment, so that wasn't a problem. With my full-time job, I asked my editor for a six-week book leave and did so after checking with and getting permission from human resources. To my surprise and disappointment, my editor said no. I didn't know why, but I knew what my response would be: I quit. It probably wasn't the smartest thing to do, especially with two small boys at home. And I had some explaining to do with my wife.

But my editor at Penguin gave the project a green light, and the only way to tell this story was to go where Sharon and Floyd had lived. And that meant traveling to Oklahoma City and Tulsa, Oklahoma; Gainesville, Tampa and Saint Petersburg, Florida; Forest Park, Georgia; and Washington, D.C., to visit with their friends and with law enforcement. It also meant prison interviews with Franklin Floyd, who had just been convicted of murder and was awaiting his transfer to death row.

To this day I have no idea why he agreed to meet with me in February 2003. And I can tell you I've never had a more disturbing interview in my career. But it was during that four-hour session that he allowed me to make copies of all of his personal documents and papers, a treasure trove he was allowed have in prison because he was acting as his own attorney. It was a fortuitous turn for me, having access to Floyd's library of information. But I could never get him to say where Sharon had come from or tell me the fate of Michael. So when the book was completed later that year I didn't have an ending. But I knew that I had a great story, and one that would tug at hearts, draw plenty of emotion, and prompt readers to react. And they did.

When the book was published in 2004, I set up an authors website with an email address for anyone who had a tip that could help in the search for Sharon's true identity. One by one, the tips came in. There were dozens, but out of all those, just a few looked promising. I sent them to Gerry Nance at the National Center for Missing & Exploited Children in Alexandria, Virginia. Gerry was a former naval investigator who handled cold cases for the National Center. We had met during my visit there while I was researching the book, and he agreed to facilitate DNA testing. We were surprised to learn that vials of Sharon's blood had been stored in Oklahoma City, where she was killed. It was originally thought to have degraded, making it useless. But as you'll read, the samples were good and her DNA was then entered into the FBI's Combined DNA Index System, or CODIS, database, which enabled Gerry and other law enforcement officials across the U.S. to compare it with potential matches.

This went on for a number of years. A couple of times we held our collective breathe, believing we had a match. We didn't.

Aside from Gerry, I remained in touch over the years with many of the law enforcement figures who played integral parts in the Sharon story, including Bob Schock and Mark Deasaro of the Saint Petersburg Police Department and Assistant U.S. Attorneys Ed Kumiega and Mark Yancy in Oklahoma City. Of course, I spoke often with retired FBI agent Joe Fitzpatrick, the hero of the book. And I traded emails with Sharon's best friend, Jenny Fisher. I was also introduced to new friends and family members, whom you'll meet in these pages.

The hope for all of us was that someday we'd learn the true identity of Sharon Marshall. But as the years passed by, that hope grew dimmer and dimmer.

It was almost ten years to the day since the publication of *A Beautiful Child* when I received an email on October 1, 2014, from Joe Fitzpatrick. "Call me," he wrote. "I have some news." Joe told me the FBI had somehow gotten Floyd to confess, and he had revealed Sharon's true identity and how she came into his custody. Joe told me her name and also shared the terrible fate of her six-year-old son, Michael.

I was stunned. That news was a long time coming, so long that I started to believe we'd never learn Sharon's true identity. But now, once it settled in, I knew I would have to find, speak to, and eventually meet members of her biological family. That would eventually include her father, a daughter and two uncles. There'd also be another best friend from high school I would meet unexpectedly while filming a program about the case in New Orleans, Louisiana. All their stories were heartbreaking.

I emailed Joe a note saying that I was going to post something on my website and on October 3, 2014, I wrote on my blog about the stunning turn of events. Readers immediately asked there and on the book's Facebook page if a sequel to *A Beautiful Child* was coming. After all, I was reminded, the book had no ending.

At first I was going to add a chapter updating *A Beautiful Child*, and my editor at Penguin, Natalee Rosenstein, was all for it. But in the spring of 2016 I flew out to Oklahoma City to speak with the FBI agents who had interviewed Floyd. Their story was remarkable, and I flew back east knowing I wasn't just adding a chapter. I also knew the focus would be on the events that transpired after the book was published in 2004. So if you haven't read it, I'd strongly suggest doing so before reading this one.

And as you do read *Finding Sharon*, there are many mentions of *A Beautiful Child*. Journalists aren't supposed to be part of the story, but this was different and I found I had to write at times in the first person. The book and its readers were the thread that kept Sharon's story alive, and after so many years that thread prompted a new review of the case. But while I may have drawn the map, it was the men and women who've dedicated their lives to serving people who did the heavy lifting, bringing resolution to a vexing case and joy to a family.

As for the title of this new book, I grappled with that long and hard. Some may ask, why Sharon? Why not her real name, which so many people put so much effort into finding?

Over the years, whenever I talked or wrote about this story, the name I always used was Sharon. And so did many others, including law enforcement officials and the National Center. It was the name she was known by during what were her happiest and most productive and successful years in the mid-1980s at Forest Park High School, and it became the de facto identifier.

Besides, the other names she used had no appeal. One name in particular, Tonya, was stolen from a tombstone in Alabama. It was also the name she was known by when she was killed, and was the name inscribed on the headstone where she was buried in Oklahoma.

I first saw that headstone during my first visit to Tulsa in 2003. It was at the Park Grove Cemetery, and I remember walking away thinking that my great hope and dream was that one day we'd learn her true identity and go back and change the name from "Tonya" to her real name. I also imagined having a ceremony, surrounded by members of her real family and friends.

As sad and tragic stories go, I finally had an ending. And this one was worth the wait.

Matt Birkbeck

February 2018

Table of Contents

Part
ONE

Chapter 1:
Mario

The cute girl rollerblading in front of an apartment complex caught the attention of a boy who couldn't keep his eyes off her.

Both were just kids, about to enter seventh grade, but the boy, whose name was Mario, was mesmerized. The girl was effortlessly skating back and forth, a smile on her face, as if she didn't have a care in the world. And she was pretty, her blond hair bouncing off her shoulders.

That was the summer of 1981, and years later, that's how Mario described his first impression of the girl he would come to know as Sharon Marshall.

It was early 2005, a few months after *A Beautiful Child* was published, when I received his email explaining that he had known Sharon so many years ago in Arizona. She was his first love, he explained, and unlike those first crushes we have as we leave childhood, this was something deep.

Mario's email was among the dozens I received from readers after the book was published. I was confident I had written a good book.

Actually, my job was to not screw it up. I had this remarkable story with so much source material, my primary responsibility was to connect the dots in such a way that readers would understand what was going on during each period of this complex, convoluted story.

Still, this was my second book and you never know how each book will be received. It was also initially published in hardcover, which is a tougher sell at twenty dollars than paperback or eBook at less than half that. And there really wasn't much in the way of promotion.

Publishers typically map out an initial schedule of interviews, TV appearances, etc. But not for this book. Few people knew the story of Sharon Marshall, so any sales and success would have to come from word of mouth. (More to the point, I never would have thought in a million years that the reader response would be such that the book would continue to sell on backlist or that it would be reprinted in several European countries or that it would lead to this sequel.)

But I had a hint at its ultimate impact by the correspondence I was receiving, via letters and, mostly, emails. Among the first was from Cathy English, the secretary/bookkeeper at Forest Park High School. She had graduated a year after Sharon, but they had been in a chemistry class together a couple of years earlier, where they had given the teacher "heck." She also worked at the local movie theater and often saw Sharon and her then boyfriend there together, always accompanied by her "father." Cathy said she felt "guilty, sickened, and just so helpless" after reading the book.

Some of the correspondence came from readers haunted by Sharon's story, and there were also emails from readers who wanted to find Sharon's true identity. Among those were people who logged into Websleuths, a website for amateurs (and others) interested in missing people.

Aside from the amateurs, I also heard from law enforcement. From San Diego, Denver, Chicago, Boston, Dallas, and even France, detective's emailed queries, some looking for specific information, while others just sought to engage.

One such email was from Richard Pike, a retired detective in Toronto who believed that Sharon could be a girl who went missing there in 1974, Cheryl Hanson. Cheryl was seven years old when she left her home in suburban Aurora, Ontario, for a short walk to her cousins' house. She was never seen again.

The Hanson tip was one of several I had passed along to Gerry Nance, who headed cold cases at the National Center for Missing & Exploited Children in suburban Washington, D.C. I had met Gerry during my visit there in 2003, and over the years he would prove to be a vital partner in the search for Sharon's identity. Through Gerry, we learned that vials of Sharon's blood taken following her death in 1990 remained in storage with the authorities in Oklahoma City. There was a question as to whether the blood had become too degraded to be of any use for DNA testing, but the blood, it turned out, was still good. So Gerry and his assistant, B.J. Spammer, now had something to use for DNA testing should a particular tip warrant further exploration. Exactly what the bar was I still can't say other than it had to be high, which meant the timing of the disappearance, the age of the missing girl, the location of Floyd at the time (he was in prison until 1973), were among the considerations.

When Richard Pike, a former law enforcement official, suggested we look into the case of Cheryl Hanson, the only question I had was placing Floyd in Canada. That aside, there was enough to warrant a DNA test. So Gerry made the arrangements for an FBI lab in Connecticut to conduct the test (with the National Center picking up the tab), and we waited. It took a few weeks, but the test came back negative.

We ended up doing this several more times over the years, with a new lead good enough to warrant a DNA test, but only to get the bad news that it wasn't a match. It was frustrating, even more so knowing that Franklin Floyd had the answers but had no intention of ever giving up his secrets. And as for Sharon's son Michael, whom Floyd had kidnapped in 1994 from his first-grade classroom in Oklahoma, the feeling among everyone associated with that case was that the boy was dead, likely killed within days after he had been taken.

I flew out to Seattle in the spring of 2005 to appear on a program there, *Northwest Afternoon*, which was devoting a full one-hour episode to the Sharon Marshall story. Video of Michael on a trip with his foster parents, Merle and Ernest Bean, was aired, with him poking his head out of an army tank. He was a cute little boy with a great smile, and it was incomprehensible that Floyd would have killed him. He had told me and others that he gave the boy to "friends" who'd promised to watch him. A part of me wanted to believe him. But I knew, having seen the sickening photos of what he did to Cheryl Commesso in 1989, that he was more than capable of something as evil as killing a little boy. And so, resigned to the likelihood that Michael was dead, I focused on finding Sharon.

Soon, emails from people who had known her and were devastated by what had happened to their friend came pouring in. These were people who simply wanted to share their remembrances of Sharon, and one was from a man who first saw her rollerblading so many years earlier.

They would meet at school, Mario wrote. They were in the same class and became fast friends. He recalled Sharon sneaking into his apartment. They'd hide in his room talking and, at times, smooching. He said his mother liked Sharon, but not Sharon's father, warning Mario to stay away from him. Mario remembered the terror-filled look in Sharon's eyes anytime she was running late at school. Her father had laid down a rule that under no circumstances was she to arrive home later than 4:00 p.m. Sharon, even as a seventh-grader, had to clean their apartment and have dinner ready.

I remembered that story all to well from her high school friends at Forest Park but had no idea it had begun years earlier.

Sharon had also told Mario how her mother had died of cancer and that her father had a bad back, how she had to give him massages. It seemed weird, but Mario knew Sharon to be a happy-go-lucky and fun girl, so the issues with her father were something of an afterthought.

It was just a year later, at the beginning of eighth grade, in 1982, when Sharon and her father suddenly moved on. No good-bye, no forwarding address. Mario was crushed and thought he'd never see Sharon Marshall again.

Several years would pass before, in the fall of 1986, Mario was at Alhambra High School's homecoming game. He was a senior and sitting in the stands with his then girlfriend and some friends when Sharon suddenly appeared. She was dressed in black and more beautiful than he had remembered. The two old friends hugged, and Sharon said she and her father had returned to the Phoenix area and she had sought Mario out, finding out from his mother that he was at the football game. Mario was stunned.

Sharon explained that she and her father had been living in Georgia, but her father's back had been acting up again and he needed to live in a region like Arizona, with low humidity. Mario ended up abandoning his girlfriend to talk with Sharon, and they spent the next few hours talking and catching up. But just like that, she was gone again, until December, when she showed up at his apartment complex riding a miniscooter. They spent that day talking. She said she was going to

Georgia Tech to study aerospace engineering. He told her he had pre-enlisted in the navy. An amateur photographer, Mario took photos of Sharon with her scooter. Her left hand and wrist were bandaged for some reason that she didn't explain.

She promised to come see him again, but like she did before, she vanished.

It wasn't until after Mario graduated high school in 1987 that he heard from Sharon again. She had sent a postcard to his mother in Phoenix saying she was living in Florida, which is where Mario was going through boot camp and attending nuclear power school for the navy. Sharon had included her phone number. Mario called her, saying they had to meet. It would take a few months, but they agreed to meet at Disney World, where they spent two days and one night—of course with her father watching over them both.

They all rode the rides together, and that night Mario and Sharon ripped off the sheets and blanket from the double bed (Floyd slept in the other one) and put them down on the balcony, where they hung out and talked. But they still weren't alone. Mario remembered her father creepily looking through the drapes to see what they were doing. Still, he had a great time.

Following the visit they continued to talk on the phone. He about his struggles with grades at navy school, while she always encouraged him. Mario never thought to ask Sharon if she was working or not. The truth, that she was a stripper at a club in Tampa and a prostitute, would have been devastating. She was also pregnant with Michael, whom she would give birth to a few months later in March. The father was another boy from Arizona, Greg Higgs.

Mario never saw Sharon again, and the phone calls stopped after a few months. But he never forgot her, even through two marriages. It was in September 2005 that he thought to look up NASA scientists on

My Space and found a Sharon Marshall and a link to *A Beautiful Child*. He immediately ordered the book and read it in a day. When he was done, he cried uncontrollably.

"I just lost it," he said. "My wife wanted to know what happened and why I was balling."

Chapter 2:

Mary

During the summer of 2005 I received a short, anonymous email. "Would the DNA of Sharon's daughter help you?"

Of the dozens of emails I received from readers with various tips, I never received one so direct and, possibly, so important.

Sharon gave birth to a daughter in New Orleans in August 1989— that much I knew. But I had no idea who the family was, who had adopted her, and whatever happened to her. So I immediately emailed back: "Yes." I included all my phone numbers and added, "Please call." Shortly after, a woman contacted me from a number with a New Orleans area code and we talked a little bit. She would only give me her first name, Mary, and we exchanged some pleasantries. She was feeling me out, but after a few minutes she felt comfortable enough to tell me her last name, Dufresne.

She explained that she had just read the book and, not wanting to disclose her identity, had asked a friend to email me. After I responded, the friend gave Mary my phone numbers, and now we were on the phone chatting.

Mary said she was the woman in the book who had adopted Sharon's daughter, but she wouldn't tell me the daughter's name. It took a few more conversations, but I finally learned her name was Megan.

Then Mary told me her story.

Mary Ann Bourgeous Dufresne had always wanted a baby of her own. An administrative assistant with the Strategic Petroleum Reserve Project, a government agency in New Orleans, Mary, like her husband, Dean, was a Cajun who enjoyed good Louisiana home cooking and good times. What was missing from their lives was a child. The young couple had tried for years to conceive a baby, even going as far as Mary taking fertility treatments. But nothing had worked, so Mary let it be known to family and friends during the summer of 1989 that she and Dean were open to adoption. Mary had been adopted, so it didn't matter how the baby arrived, so long as they could share their lives with a child.

It wasn't long after word got out that Mary received a phone call from a friend who was a secretary at a local attorney's office. A man and a young woman had just left the office, she said, and the woman was pregnant and they were looking to give the baby up for adoption.

"Would you be interested?" said the friend.

"Of course I am, definitely," Mary replied.

A meeting was scheduled at the attorney's office and Mary and Dean were introduced to Clarence Hughes, his wife, Tonya, and their son, Michael. Tonya was young, around twenty years old, and he was much older, perhaps in his forties. The boy was about one year old, maybe a few months older. Clarence did all the talking. He explained that they couldn't afford to raise another child, so they wanted to give the baby up for adoption. Tonya kept her head down and remained quiet during the entire meeting, with the exception of holding, tickling, and kissing Michael.

Clarence said there was a price for the baby, $10,000. Mary's attorney explained that Louisiana had rules and regulations for adoptions, which allowed for the payments for living expenses the month before, the month of, and the month after the birth. The Dufresnes agreed to pay $1,000 for each of the three months as well as for all doctor's visits and medical bills. Total payments would come to slightly over $7,000. Clarence grudgingly accepted the offer.

Mary asked her attorney to get whatever background information he could on the Hughes family, which would amount to copies of their valid driver's licenses.

Tonya was due in nine weeks, they said, so the expectation was she'd give birth in September. She had yet to see a gynecologist, so appointments were made for Tonya with a local doctor, and Mary would accompany Tonya for each visit. But whenever Mary arrived, she was met by Clarence, and when Tonya's name was called, Clarence would follow her and Mary into the examination room.

It was during those visits that Mary would see and get to play with Michael. Tonya wasn't very talkative and typically kept her head down whenever she was with Clarence, which was all the time. Tonya was clearly afraid of her much older husband, who did all the talking with the doctor. Tonya perked up when she held Michael. She adored her son. But obviously not Clarence, who never left her alone with anyone, with one exception.

It was August 11, 1989, and Mary got the call that Tonya's water had broken. The baby was coming several weeks earlier than expected. By the time Mary got to the hospital, Tonya had given birth to a daughter at 4:59 p.m. Both Tonya and the baby were well, and Mary was beyond excited. When she walked into Tonya's room, she was surprised to find her alone. Clarence was off somewhere talking to the doctors, so Mary seized on the rare opportunity.

"Did you see the baby?"

"No, not really. They just took her away."

"Do you want to see her?"

"No, I don't."

"Are you sure?"

"Yes."

"I want you to understand that, even though you're giving the baby up for adoption and don't want to see her now, if you ever change your mind in the future you are welcome to contact us," said Mary.

Tonya declined the invitation. She was sad, very sad, and the short conversation quickly ended when Clarence entered the room. When Mary arrived the next day, Tonya was gone. She had been discharged earlier that morning. She and Clarence had signed the release papers, and Mary took her new daughter home the next day. Mary named her Megan.

A few weeks later Mary and Dean met one last time with Clarence, Tonya, and Michael at their attorney's office to sign off on more forms as well as submit the final $1,000. Clarence and Tonya had six months to change their minds. Mary never saw or heard from them again.

Mary treasured her new daughter, and her life was now complete.

It was a few years later, in the summer of 1994, when Mary received a call from the Oklahoma Department of Human Services in Oklahoma City, asking if she'd be interested in adopting Michael Hughes. The caseworker there explained that Michael's mother, Tonya, had died in a car accident in 1990 and Michael had been placed in foster care.

Mary remembered the little boy and said, yes, she was interested, but she needed more information. What happened to the father, Clarence, and how was Michael doing with his foster family?

She was taken aback when she was told that the man she had met, Clarence Hughes, was really a federal fugitive named Franklin Delano Floyd. He was an ex-con who had been on the run since 1973 after violating his parole. And his young wife, whom Mary knew as Tonya? No one knew much about her other than that wasn't her real name. The caseworker said that after Tonya died, Floyd was imprisoned for two years for violating his parole back in 1973. Upon his release he sought custody of Michael, but a DNA test revealed that he wasn't the boy's biological father. That didn't deter Floyd, who filed custody petitions with the courts arguing that he had raised Michael from birth. Floyd's legal challenge put a hold on the effort of Michael's foster parents, Merle and Ernest Bean, to adopt him.

The Beans lived in Choctaw, just outside of Oklahoma City. They were simple, churchgoing people who opened their home to a host of children. Michael was sent there in 1990 after his mother was killed and Floyd went to prison. When Michael arrived, he was emotionally stunted and cried all the time. But by 1994, he had become a happy little boy who fished with Ernest and sang at church with the rest of the family. He was also about to begin first grade.

With the Beans caught in legal limbo, someone at DHS thought it was a good idea to reach out to Mary to see if she'd be interested in adopting Michael. Mary was horrified by the story, and she had no idea how DHS in Oklahoma had found her. She was even more befuddled after someone anonymously sent her the result of Floyd's DNA test. Mary presumed it was someone at DHS again. She wanted Michael, but she was told how the Beans had done a remarkable job and wanted to adopt him. Mary ultimately decided that it wouldn't be wise or kind to remove Michael from such a loving home, and she said no. Let the Beans adopt him, she said, but she'd be very open to meeting with them and providing regular contact between Michael and his little sister, Megan, after the Beans formalized the adoption.

Everything changed in mid-September 1994, when two FBI agents arrived at Mary's house in New Orleans. Floyd had lost his final appeal and then, incredibly, had kidnapped Michael at gunpoint from his first-grade classroom two days earlier, they said. In going through personal documents found at Floyd's apartment in Oklahoma City, the FBI had found the paperwork for Megan's adoption, which led them to Mary.

The first questions from the FBI agents centered on determining if Mary and her husband were involved.

"Of course we're not," said Mary. "I'd take a lie detector test to prove it."

A test wasn't necessary, they said. They believed her. But there was another concern.

"We think he could be heading in this direction," they said. "We're also going to have to go to Megan's school and talk to the officials. Floyd could show up there."

The agents left, and Mary was relieved when she received calls from DHS and the U.S. Marshals office six weeks later saying that Floyd had been captured in Louisville, Kentucky. But Michael was gone.

The story was beyond bizarre and terribly sad and frightening. So Mary made a point of keeping secret the origin of Megan's adoption, especially after *Unsolved Mysteries* aired a program on the kidnapping of Michael Hughes in 1997. Several years later, in 2002, Mary read how Floyd had been convicted of murdering a young woman, Cheryl Commesso, in Saint Petersburg, Florida, in 1989. He had been using the name Warren Marshall, and Tonya was then known as his daughter, Sharon Marshall. Sometime between fleeing Saint Petersburg and arriving in New Orleans, they had changed their names to Clarence and Tonya Hughes and then married.

By late 2004 a website called Websleuths began posting group chats about a book called *A Beautiful Child* as well as subchats about Franklin Floyd, Sharon Marshall, and Michael Hughes. The amateur detectives, or "sleuthers," as they were known, threw out different theories on Sharon's real identity, as well as the fate of her son, Michael.

It was in 2005 when a friend told Mary about the book and that it told the story of Franklin Floyd and Sharon Marshall. Mary got it the next day and read it in one sitting, as did her husband. They were shocked, angry, sad, and horrified. Mary was also scared and relieved. She realized that if she and Dean had adopted Michael, Floyd would have come to New Orleans, and who knows what he would have done. At the least, Mary knew she and her family would have been in danger. Mary also had a new concern.

The book revealed how Sharon, then known as Tonya, had given up a baby for adoption in New Orleans. There were several details, including how much had been paid to Floyd, but no mention of who had adopted the baby or the baby's name.

Mary had over the years kept a close eye on the media and Internet see if their secret had been revealed. It hadn't, until now. This was the first time there had been any mention of a New Orleans connection, and she was worried. Her concerns grew after a friend who regularly logged onto Websleuths told Mary that some of the sleuthers had announced they were going to try to find the baby who had been given up for adoption in New Orleans.

Mary asked the friend to email me. After confiding that her daughter's name was Megan, Mary told me that Megan was a student in high school. She was a straight-A student, played varsity volleyball, and planned to go to college to study athletic training at Southeastern Louisiana University.

Megan sounded just like Sharon, and I was thrilled. I broached the idea of a DNA test. I told her that the Oklahoma City Police Department still had vials of Sharon's blood, taken when she died, and that I was working with someone at the National Center who could facilitate a test. I had no reason not to believe Mary, but the test would put away any doubts as to the validity of Sharon's blood. Mary said yes, and I called Gerry Nance, who readily agreed. A swab was taken from Megan's mouth and sent to the lab. There was some concern that Sharon's blood had degraded to the point of being useless. But six weeks later Gerry called with the happy result: we had a match.

So now we could use Megan's DNA if we had to. But we still had to find Sharon's birth family.

Chapter 3:
Ray Baby

Lynn Rene Thornton couldn't take it anymore.

Virtually the entirety of his time as a student at Forest Park High School, he had been cursed at, physically abused, and called a "faggot" and other homophobic and hurtful names.

A shy, skinny, handsome teenager with a mop of blond hair, Lynn was the son of a woman who was a criminal investigator for the Atlanta Police Department. His birth father, a uranium miner, didn't want anything to do with him. Lynn later had a stepfather who wanted to adopt him, but who also beat him regularly, even breaking a few bones.

For as long as Lynn could remember, life had been a struggle. Even something as simple as eating. Not that he couldn't put food down — there just wasn't much of it in his household. His mother had a job, but it didn't pay well. Things got so desperate he was sent to the Georgia Baptist Children's home and attended school there for third and fourth grade.

Later, when he reached his teens, Lynn and his mother, Barbara, moved to Forest Park, which was among the least expensive neighborhoods in the Atlanta area, and he registered at the local high school.

Almost every day there nearly brought him to tears.

During one particularly bad day, after a group of students laughed as they shoved him into his locker, he was sitting by himself on the front steps of the high school when he noticed a strikingly beautiful girl staring at him.

Lynn looked away, but when he turned his head back he saw she was walking towards him.

"Hi, I'm Sharon," she said.

Lynn awkwardly said hello back, and as he was about to say his name, she stopped him.

"I know your name."

"You do?"

"Yes. I watch. I look around."

Sharon said she knew Lynn was a sophomore.

"I'm a junior," she said.

Sharon wasn't just beautiful; she was confident and spoke like someone who was much older. She also had a great smile and made him feel at ease.

The two became friends immediately, and that friendship quickly blossomed. Sharon called him "Ray Baby." There was no reason for it. She just liked it. Lynn never had a friend as beautiful or smart as Sharon or one who had taken such an interest in him.

At school Sharon was always smiling and always carried books in her arms. She would write notes and pass them to Lynn in the hallway and laugh and joke with him. Some students gossiped that they were dating.

Sharon became Lynn's angel and made his existence at school tolerable. She'd yell at other students and defend her friend whenever they verbally abused him, often sticking her finger in their faces and yelling, "Leave him alone!"

And she was enraged when her Ray Baby told her that his counselor said he wasn't college material. She took her friend aside.

"No, don't listen to him," she said. "You can do anything you put your mind to."

Sharon's faith in Lynn filled him with a strength he never thought he had. The other kids had noticed to the point where the taunting had been limited from an everyday occurrence to perhaps once in a while.

After school, Lynn sat in the stands and watched as Sharon led her Air Force ROTC class through drills. She had that drive, and marching in her uniform, she looked like she belonged in the military.

Lynn loved his new friend. Not sexually. He had known for a long time that he was attracted to other boys. But his love for Sharon was deep, from his heart. He felt great comfort being with Sharon, and she with him. And even after Sharon told him about her new friend Jennifer.

"I have a best girlfriend. She has a nice house on the other side of town," she said with a spark in her eye.

Lynn was happy for Sharon, but he also had concerns, specifically with her father.

From time to time he'd walk Sharon home from school, but never enter the small, nondescript house near the end of the block. Instead they'd sit on her front porch and talk. Every now and then she'd talk about her father, Warren. She had to be home by 4:00 p.m. every day to clean the house and feed her father, she said. He was a painter and had a bad back.

But during one conversation, Sharon appeared distraught.

"What's wrong," he said

"I couldn't sleep last night. My dad works so hard. He comes into my room and says he's hurting, so I have to give him a massage."

"Your dad forces you to give him massages?"

"Yeah," she said, before leaning over to hug Lynn.

"Don't worry, everything will be fine," he whispered.

But things weren't fine.

During his junior year, Lynn thought he'd try modeling. He had a photographer take some headshots, and they were good enough to secure an agent. Soon after, Sharon began passing him her own photos. Her father was an amateur photographer, she said. Lynn thought some of the photos were a bit too sexy. Sharon began asking about his agent and whether he could pass her photos along. Lynn said sure, figuring her dad had gotten ahold of his headshot and résumé.

She then told him that her father wanted him to accompany them to a studio where he could take photos of them together. Sharon said her father wanted to expand his portfolio. They picked Lynn up on a Saturday in Warren's pickup truck and drove to a crime-ridden warehouse district and pulled up to a decrepit building. Warren told Sharon and Lynn to wait in the truck, and he walked inside. Twenty minutes later, he walked back to the truck.

"This fucking place isn't going to work. We can't do it here," he said.

Warren was angry, and Lynn was scared. Sharon could see the fear in Lynn's face and she looked directly into his eyes to calm him down.

"Don't worry, Ray Baby. We'll be OK," she said.

A week later, Sharon and Lynn were studying together at Lynn's apartment when suddenly there was a loud bang at the door.

"Sharon, you get out here now!"

It was Warren, and he kept yelling while banging on the door.

Lynn's mother, Barbara, was still in her police uniform with a gun in her holster when she opened the door.

"I want Sharon and I want her now!" Warren demanded.

Sharon quickly gathered her things and left. Lynn's mom was concerned.

"What was that?" she said. "I don't ever want you over at her house again. Ever. Do you understand me?"

Lynn told his mother about the drive to the warehouse for the unsettling photo shoot and that Sharon gave her father massages.

Barbara's experience with the Atlanta Police Department set off every alarm and panic button in her being.

"I want you to listen to me," she said. "You do not go over there."

Lynn asked if there was anything she could do. Barbara wanted to help, but she said that unless Sharon said directly that her father was molesting her, she couldn't do anything.

Lynn did what his mother had asked and he had no interaction with Warren. But that didn't stop Warren from to trying to reschedule the photo shoot. Sharon would ask and Lynn would say no. But Lynn noticed that Sharon wouldn't try to change his mind. She was actually *relieved* that he'd back out, as if she knew something bad would happen and she was trying to protect him. Sharon would never admit to it, but Lynn knew her well enough to know something wasn't right. And he became concerned with her welfare, even more so when she told him she was pregnant.

During Sharon's senior year she wore more makeup and sexier, tighter fitting clothing, often showing her shoulders and cleavage. Some students began calling her a slut and a whore. She had a boyfriend, but on dates her father would always accompany her. Some teachers at Forest Park became concerned, and they quietly speculated whether her father was molesting her.

As the school year progressed, Sharon gained weight and by the spring it was obvious to everyone that she was pregnant.

Lynn didn't see much of Sharon then. Instead, they'd talk on the phone a couple of times a week. Just before her graduation, Sharon suggested he go to summer school. Since his grades had improved to college level, he could graduate early, she said.

Weeks went by before the two friends spoke again. It was midsummer when Lynn picked up the phone and, to his shock, heard Sharon's voice.

"Where have you been?" he said. "It's been, what, two months since I heard from you!"

"Oh, I'm living in this apartment with this guy," she said.

There was yelling in the background.

"Who's that?" said Lynn.

"That's just my dad. He's living with us. Someone has to take care of him with his back and all."

Lynn was startled that Sharon was still with her father, and even worse living with him. She wouldn't tell Lynn where she was, or anything about the baby.

"Can I come visit you?"

"No, I don't think that's a good idea right now," she said.

Lynn told her he had taken her advice and was attending summer school. He was going to graduate high school early, in December, and had been admitted to Shorter College in Rome, Georgia, where he would study for a bachelor's degree in voice and piano. And the best news was, he'd be going on scholarship.

"Oh my God, you did it. You got into college! And you got a scholarship? I knew you could do it!"

"Well, I couldn't have done it without you. You know that," he said. "You gave me the confidence to succeed."

"No, no, no. It was you. You always had it in you," she said. "I'm so proud of you, Ray Baby!"

The two friends said good-bye, with Sharon promising to call.

But they would never speak again.

Thirty years would pass before Lynn would share his story.

Chapter 4:

The Counselor

Jean Gaissert had been a student counselor at Forest Park High School for two years when she was asked to have a word with Sharon Marshall.

Gaissert wasn't Sharon's official adviser, but she knew her from ROTC. Gaissert was an adviser with the program and had traveled to the Air Force Academy in Colorado with other educators to learn more about the air force.

Sharon, now a senior, had been nominated for a four-year ROTC scholarship to Georgia Tech. Everyone congratulated her in January 1986 upon hearing the news, and all she had to do was keep her sterling grades up until graduation and pass a physical.

But a rumor about Sharon began floating through the school that spring, and her counselor, a single man, approached Gaissert, believing she was better equipped to discuss the matter with Sharon.

"Can you do me a favor," he said. "I know she's not your student, but can you talk to Sharon Marshall about a rumor that she's pregnant? I just don't feel comfortable with this."

Gaissert thought about it and, yes, she had noticed during ROTC drills that Sharon had gained a little weight. But it wasn't just the pregnancy that was bothering her colleague. There were the other rumors, and they concerned Sharon and her strange, demanding father.

He had been to the school several times over the years to talk with Sharon's counselors, and all thought he was very odd. He'd come to talk about Sharon and her progress, but wasn't forthcoming when asked questions. The faculty and students knew that Sharon had to be home by 4:00 p.m. every day to care for him and how she'd become tense and even erratic if she didn't leave on time. There was also the chatter about the differing claims about the cause of her mother's death, either from cancer or a car accident. But perhaps most unsettling was that her father would drive Sharon to school every morning and when he dropped her off they would kiss on the mouth when saying good-bye. Some were questioning whether, if she *was* pregnant, her father might be the father of her baby.

And as if that weren't enough, there was another issue, unrelated to her father. Sharon had to pass a year-end physical to gain final approval for the ROTC scholarship, and if she was pregnant, the scholarship would be rescinded.

"I think you need to talk to her, if you can," the other counselor said.

Gaissert agreed and called Sharon into her office and sat her down.

"Sharon, I know you don't know me very well, but there's something we need to know about and address," Gaissert said. "There's a rumor going around that you're pregnant."

Sharon blithely deflected the question. "I don't know why that rumor is going around," she said. "I just gained a little weight."

"That's OK. But look, I'm not going to accuse you of anything, but if you *are* pregnant you're not going to get the ROTC scholarship," Gaissert said.

"Well, I'm not pregnant," said Sharon defiantly before leaving the office.

Despite her denials, the rumor persisted, and a month later a representative from the ROTC visited with Gaissert to express concern.

"She's not pregnant," Gaissert assured her, "but I'll call her again."

In mid-April, with graduation day fast approaching, Gaissert again summoned Sharon.

"Listen, that rumor is persisting and keeps going around and I really need to know if you're pregnant or not," Gaissert said.

Sharon, who'd been slightly annoyed the first time she was ordered to the office, was now visibly irritated.

"I wish everybody would just mind their own business," she snapped. "I'm *not* pregnant, and I'm tired of all this."

"I understand that, I really do," said Gaissert. "But the situation with the ROTC scholarship is such that if you were pregnant, we'd like to give it to another student."

Sharon didn't respond and remained silent until Gaissert told her she could leave.

The counselor then went to the principal and explained that she'd done everything she could and they'd now have to wait until September, when Sharon was expected to begin her studies at Georgia Tech.

Sharon was AWOL at her graduation ceremony, and by midsummer she and her father had vanished. The new rumor swirling around Forest Park was that she'd gone to Arkansas, given birth to her baby, and then married her daddy.

Chapter 5:
Heather

When Heather first saw Sharon Marshall, she couldn't get over how cute she was.

Heather was a manager at the Mons Venus club in Tampa, Florida, a premier strip club with a niche clientele that included wealthy foreigners, famous actors, and athletes. The girls who danced there were not only beautiful, but also respectful and smart. Many earned over $1,000 per night, and some invested their money in the stock market and real estate.

Heather had arrived in 1987. She was blonde, beautiful, and, despite her youth, she was already a seasoned veteran of the club scene. Heather danced, became a manager, and even turned tricks on the side. She never used a last name, only "Heather," and she was a lighting rod at the Mons, a bisexual mother of sorts. The other girls always clung to her, seeking advice about things inside and outside the club. Money, boyfriends, sex, careers, whatever. If they had a question or a problem, they went to Heather.

When Sharon first arrived at the Mons, she was a little doll with ringlets in her hair, wore a tight skirt and bobby socks. She was sexy, but also had innocence about her, which Heather knew would be attractive to the club's patrons. And when Heather hired Sharon and put her up on the Mons stage, her instinct proved correct. Sharon was a hit. She was so good, it masked the disdain that nearly everyone had for her father, Warren.

Warren was a weird duck who'd drive his daughter to work every night. At first, he'd come into the club to watch Sharon dance. But that was deemed too creepy by club management, so he'd remain outside in the parking lot until Sharon's shift ended. During breaks, Sharon would read one of the books or magazines she always carried with her or go out to the car and have a snack, talk to her father, and play with her baby son, Michael, who would remain strapped into a child seat.

The dynamic was strange and unsettling. But Warren was engaging, often talking with the other dancers and offering support for their career choice. He made them feel good about working in an industry on which others didn't look so favorably. Some of the girls, including Heather, even heeded his wish to be called "Dad."

Heather and Sharon became friends, and as the months passed by they'd often talk backstage. One conversation centered on Heather's other work outside Mons, where she'd meet clients for sex, usually at a high-end hotel. Sharon asked if she could come along.

"I never thought you were that type of girl," said Heather. "I thought you were so innocent and not someone looking to do private parties and all that goes with it."

Sharon said she was game and, besides, had done it before. Heather said yes. The following week, the two women scheduled their first party together. Sharon agreed to pick up Heather at her apartment, and as she waited outside, a car pulled up, but Warren was driving. Sharon and Michael were in the backseat. Warren said he wanted to accompany them to the hotel. When they arrived, he reached into his pocket and pulled out several condoms, gave them to Sharon, and then waited in the car with Michael as the girls entered the hotel.

Roughly an hour had passed when they returned to the car.

Warren appeared excited, mostly over the money they were making. On the return drive back to Heather's he praised them both for being willing to do that kind of work. He then asked Heather, for the next party, if could go inside and watch. He said he wanted to take pictures. Heather was taken aback and said no. Warren, she knew, was not your average father. And Sharon wasn't so innocent after all. Having watched Sharon have sex, Heather could see her new friend knew how to please a man.

From then on the routine was always the same: Warren drove them to and from their private parties, and with Heather taking the front passenger seat he'd always strike up a conversation while Sharon remained quiet in the back with Michael. One night, Warren reached over into the backseat, grabbed Sharon's breast, and pinched her nipple. She grimaced, having just had breast implant surgery.

"Look at these. She finally got a boob job," he said with a hint of satisfaction. "And now all she just needs is to get into porn. She's all ready."

Warren asked Heather if she knew anyone in the adult entertainment business.

"I'd like Sharon to get into porn," he said.

Heather said she didn't know anyone who could help. She also wondered to herself about the total control that Warren had over his daughter.

The following week, Sharon surprised Heather with a request.

"One of my dad's friends is coming to town. Will you come with me?"

Heather said sure, but regretted it the moment she arrived. This wasn't one of the upscale hotels they frequented. Instead, it was a seedy motel in a remote part of town. When they knocked on the door to the room, a middle-aged man was waiting. Sharon introduced them, and the man told Heather he was a lifelong friend of Sharon's father and that he had been having sex with Sharon most of her life.

The man then undressed and watched as Sharon and Heather simulated lesbian acts. Heather then sat on the side of the bed as Sharon had sex with him.

Not long afterward, they had their final party together. Warren drove as usual and, as he did whenever they talked, he reiterated his support of her career choices. But then Heather mentioned something about bondage and spanking, and Warren suddenly became overly excited.

"You know, if you are into that kind of thing, I can horse fuck you! And if you don't believe me, just ask Sharon!"

Warren couldn't stop talking about it. The mere mention of sexually violent acts had set him off. Sharon said nothing. She was, as usual, very quiet, numb even. Heather became ill. Unbeknownst to Warren or Sharon, Heather had had her own personal experience with a sexually violent man, having been kidnapped at the age of nine by a convicted rapist and held against her will by him for five years.

When Warren dropped her off at the Mons, Heather ran inside. She told security she never wanted to see Warren Marshall again. He was sick and highly manipulative, she said. Heather had seen the same pattern from her kidnapper, but she was so duped by Warren she had missed it, until now. She was also convinced that Warren was having sex with Sharon. Heather became so upset, she began to tell others about Sharon and that her father was molesting her. She also told them about the health of Sharon's son, Michael. The little boy, only six months old, clearly had developmental disabilities. He could hardly hold his head up, and the back of his head was almost flat, likely from sitting in his car seat for hours on end, Heather surmised. Perhaps he was even retarded, she said to the other dancers.

Sharon eventually heard the rumors and ran to Heather, unaware that it was Heather who had started them.

"Everyone thinks your dad is crazy," Heather responded. "They also think you should take Michael and leave him. Get far away from him and start a new life. There are people here who will help you."

Sharon was terrified.

"I can't do that," she cried.

"Why not?" Heather asked.

"You don't understand," said Sharon, now trembling, her voice at a whisper. "He's not my real father. He's my stepfather. He's been molesting me and raping me most of my life. He doesn't do it anymore. But he did it for most of my life."

Tears began to flow down Sharon's cheeks, and Heather was sympathetic.

"You have to get out of this, this relationship," she said. "This is dangerous for you, and it's sickening. It's also sickening for all of your friends and coworkers to see."

Sharon's demeanor quickly changed from tearful to terrified.

"You can't tell anyone," she begged. "He'll kill me. He will kill me. You don't understand. I have Michael now, and he never leaves him, my dad. He has him all the time. Please, please don't tell anyone."

Heather said she'd remain quiet, and she did, even after Sharon came to say good-bye.

It was spring 1989, and Sharon was pregnant again, she said. The father was a nice college boy she was seeing on the side. They'd meet every morning for breakfast to talk, usually about books.

But now, they were leaving. Sharon said she, her son, and her father were heading out west. The move was sudden and came out of nowhere, but there was nothing she could do about it. Heather listened as Sharon tried to explain, but her mind was elsewhere. Heather's attention was with another friend, Cheryl Commesso, who hadn't reported to work at the Mons in several days and no one had heard from her.

Heather gave Sharon a hug, and the two women never saw each other again.

Franklin Floyd (a.k.a. Warren Marshall) and Sharon, early 1980s.

Sharon (second from right) receiving Math award at Forest Park High School during Honors' Night, May 7, 1985. (Photo courtesy of Jean Gaissert).

Sharon (bottom, second from right), receiving ROTC Award, May 7, 1985.
(Photo courtesy of Jean Gaissert).

Sharon (top left and bottom) at Forest Park High School's Military Ball, February 15, 1986. A Lt. Colonel in the Air Force ROTC, she was selected to receive the high school's ROTC college scholarship and attend Georgia Tech. (Photo courtesy of Jean Gaissert).

"Ray Baby" Lynn (Thornton) Clemons. High school graduation, June 1987.
Sharon's support and encouragement helped him survive high school, and graduate from college.
(Photo courtesy of Lynn Clemons).

*After leaving Georgia, Sharon returned to Phoenix in the fall of 1986
and surprised her friend Mario at a Homecoming game.*
(Photo by Mario)

Sharon with her scooter surprising Mario with a visit in Phoenix, December 1986.
(Photo by Mario)

Sharon at Disney World, fall 1987.
(Photo by Mario).

Mario's last photo of Sharon on the balcony outside their room at Disney World, fall 1987.
(Photo by Mario).

Part TWO

Chapter 6:
Meeting Floyd

The early morning sun glared through the windshield and into the eyes of FBI agents Scott Lobb and Nate Furr, who sat in a car parked in a lot outside the Union Correctional Facility, near Gainesville, Florida.

The two agents had the day before boarded a flight to Florida from their home bureau in Oklahoma City and then drove one hour from their hotel to the maximum security prison, where, on this hot morning, they were sitting in their rental car anticipating the difficult task at hand: interviewing Franklin Delano Floyd.

Floyd had been on death row at the prison since February 2003 following his conviction for the 1989 murder of nineteen-year-old Cheryl Commesso. Commesso was a dancer at the Mons Venus, a strip joint in Tampa that was a favorite hangout for professional athletes and rock stars. Floyd had sadistically beaten and sexually tortured the teenager and then killed her by firing two bullets into the back of her head before dumping her body off Interstate 195 in Saint Petersburg.

But the agents hadn't traveled to Gainesville to talk about Commesso. The meeting was about Commesso's friend Sharon Marshall.

In 2011, the National Center for Missing & Exploited Children, also known as NCMEC, decided to take another look at the Sharon Marshall case. A young forensic investigator, Ashley Rodriquez, was given the assignment.

Sharon, as she was known at the National Center, was a young woman who had been struck by a car and killed off a highway in Oklahoma City in 1990. The coroner had ruled her death a homicide and her husband was a suspect, but no one was ever arrested.

At the time of her death she was known as Tonya Tadlock Hughes and lived with her husband, Clarence, and their two-year-old son, Michael, in Tulsa, where she danced at a strip club called Passions. Following her death, it was revealed that Tonya wasn't her real name. Clarence, was actually a federal fugitive on the run since 1973. His real name was Franklin Delano Floyd, and after completing a ten-year sentence for robbing a bank, he violated his parole and traveled the country under assumed names. With him was a young girl, who also went by many names and whom he had raised as his daughter. One of her assumed names was Sharon Marshall.

Following his release from prison in March 1993, Floyd sought custody of Sharon's son, Michael, who had been assigned to foster parents, Ernest and Merle Bean, following Sharon's death. Floyd claimed he was Michael's biological father, but DNA testing proved otherwise. After being turned away by the courts in his attempts to gain custody of Michael, Floyd kidnapped the boy at gunpoint from his first-grade classroom at Choctaw Elementary School in September 1994.

Floyd was on the run once more but was captured six weeks later in Louisville, Kentucky. Michael was gone and would never be seen again. Floyd would later be convicted and sentenced to fifty-five years in prison. It was during his federal kidnapping trial in 1995 that a mechanic in Kansas, who had purchased the truck Floyd stole during the kidnapping, discovered a large envelope taped underneath the pickup. Inside the envelope were more than 100 lurid pictures of Sharon and other little girls, along with graphic photos of a young woman being beaten and tortured. It was Cheryl Commesso. Floyd was tried for her murder in 2001, found guilty, and sentenced to death.

Ashley Rodriquez had joined the National Center in 2008 as an assistant case manager in the missing-children division and mostly worked on cases involving runaways. In November 2011, the forensic services unit at the National Center started a program that would focus on unidentified juvenile remains. Rodriguez was transferred to that unit and given a caseload that included the "Sharon Marshall" case.

The National Center had only a brief file on Sharon Marshall, which mostly included tips that had been forwarded to Gerry Nance, a cold-case investigator who had retired in 2010. In early 2012, a supervisor at the National Center gave Rodriguez a copy of *A Beautiful Child* to read.

The National Center's files didn't contain much on Sharon Marshall, and the book was Rodriquez's first exposure to the case. It also alerted her to former FBI agent Joe Fitzpatrick, who had led the investigation into the kidnapping of Michael Hughes.

Rodriguez wanted to talk to Fitzpatrick, so she reached out to the FBI liaisons at the National Center. They connected her to Fitzpatrick, who had retired from the FBI but was more than happy to speak to Rodriguez. Fitzpatrick told her there had never been an official FBI investigation of the Sharon Marshall case; his focus had been finding her son, Michael. It was Fitzpatrick who had captured Floyd weeks after the kidnapping in Louisville, Kentucky.

Struck by Sharon's story, Fitzpatrick spent years on his own time investigating and trying to find her real identity and family but hit dead ends.

Fitzpatrick was happy to talk about Sharon Marshall and readily agreed to help Rodriguez, who then reached out to the Oklahoma City FBI bureau to see if they would be interested in taking another look at Sharon Marshall with the help of the National Center.

The FBI agreed and sent two agents to the Comprehensive Case Review symposium Rodriquez organized at National Center headquarters in Alexandria, Virginia, on November 13–14, 2012. Fitzpatrick was also flown in and joined the agents as well as members of the FBI's Behavioral Analysis Unit, NCIS, several other federal agencies, and National Center officials from various units.

During those meetings, the FBI agents from Oklahoma City shared their entire file on the Michael Hughes case. By the time the symposium was over, the group had shaped a tentative strategy that focused on Franklin Delano Floyd. The plan was to interview Floyd.

Back in Oklahoma City, the case was handed over to another agent, Scott Lobb.

A former agent with the U.S. Border Patrol, Lobb had been with the FBI for twelve years, the last four in Oklahoma City as the Crimes Against Children coordinator. It was, within the Oklahoma City FBI bureau, a natural landing spot for a review of the Sharon Marshall case.

But Lobb knew nothing about Sharon Marshall, and he had just begun to read the forty-five-page summary of the National Center meetings, written by Ashley Rodriquez, when she called asking for his thoughts.

"Give me a couple of days to figure what you're talking about," said Lobb. He went to his supervisor, who told him to spend time on the case only when he wasn't busy. But Lobb dove in. He finished the National Center summary and then read *A Beautiful Child*, which the FBI had on file. Like many other readers, Lobb was hooked on the case after reading the book.

In June 2013, Ashley Rodriguez flew to Oklahoma City to meet with Lobb and strategize. She promised the full cooperation of the National Center. Lobb's initial strategy was to follow the recommendations from the National Center meeting the previous November, which suggested an interview with Franklin Floyd.

Before he'd do that, though, Lobb told Rodriguez he was going to contact Joe Fitzpatrick, whose fingerprints were all over the case. Fitzpatrick agreed to meet, and the two men were introduced at an Oklahoma City fast food restaurant. For nearly three hours Fitzpatrick shared his thoughts, mostly about how he believed that Floyd would never give up Sharon's identity.

Floyd was clearly a sick individual. He had kidnapped Sharon when she was a toddler, sometime in the early to mid-1970s, subjecting her over the years to psychological terror compounded by frequent sexual assaults. A federal fugitive, Floyd believed the FBI was trailing him, and he regularly moved from state to state. Lobb didn't see any clear route in which an interview would produce a confession.

Fitzpatrick did have some advice.

"Let him go, let Floyd rant," said Fitzpatrick.

To that end, Lobb had an idea.

Special Agent Nate Furr was the interrogation instructor at the FBI's Oklahoma City bureau. He had spent ten years as a police officer in Arkansas before joining the FBI in 2009. Lobb and Furr were friends, and when Lobb approached him in January 2014, he specifically asked how he would go about preparing for an interview with someone like a Franklin Floyd. There is a science to conducting interviews, for which all FBI agents were trained for. But Lobb knew that Furr was an expert and realized that, with the challenge at hand, he needed someone there to offer him criticism. He needed help.

A few days later, Lobb dropped *A Beautiful Child* on Furr's desk. After he read it, Furr walked over to Lobb's office.

"OK, you got me," said Furr.

The interrogation instructor devised a plan in which the two agents would sift through every resource they could find, from the book to their own case files to TV interviews with Floyd that were posted on YouTube. They wanted to understand what made Floyd tick. Thousands of documents, dating back to 1965, were laid out on the floor in Furr's home.

They also listened to Floyd's few jailhouse phone calls, which had been recorded, and watched video of Floyd when he appeared before the Oklahoma legislature in the early 1990s pleading for custody of Michael. They wanted to see how he operated, how he worked. They knew he was a master manipulator and were also aware of his phenomenal memory. If you asked the same question posed by other interviewers years earlier, Floyd would give the same answer.

"We just have to keep him out of gutters, keep him down the middle," said Furr. "When someone rambles, there's a lot of leakage. We're hoping for leakage. And when we go in, we want to control the chaos."

The plan was to spend a few months researching Floyd and then, later in the year, actually fly to Florida to interview him. But in early 2014 Lobb received a call from Fitzpatrick, who said he was being interviewed for an Investigation Discovery channel program on the Sharon Marshall case. Fitzpatrick suggested that if Floyd saw the program before meeting with the FBI agents, he could feel emboldened with the new publicity he'd received and lose his incentive to talk.

Lobb called Ashley Rodriguez at the National Center and told her what Fitzpatrick had said. Both agreed that the interview with Floyd should be conducted as soon as possible.

Lobb then went to his supervisor and relayed Fitzpatrick's concerns.

"Here's my thoughts," said Lobb. "Floyd may get to see this and he's going to get some notoriety. Now's the time."

The supervisor agreed, and the interview was targeted for mid-May. That would allow Lobb's supervisor to seek budget approval for the travel to Florida and cut through any bureaucratic red tape, specifically with the prison and the notification to the local FBI office there that the Oklahoma City bureau was sending two agents to conduct an interview.

Their calendar shortened, Lobb and Furr pressed harder and consolidated their research and strategy schedule. They left Oklahoma City on Monday, May 26, and the next morning, after months of preparation, they exited the car and were about to enter the prison to talk to a death row inmate who hadn't had a visitor in years.

Chapter 7:
A Confession

The sparse furniture in the interview room at the Union Correctional Institution had to be repositioned. First to be moved was a table next to a long, soundproof window, which was built into the cinder-block wall. The window offered a view into the hallway, where other inmates and prison personnel walked by.

Nate Furr's interview strategy necessitated pushing the table against the back wall, while a wooden chair was placed in front of the window and just a few inches from another chair reserved for Franklin Floyd.

Scott Lobb would sit next to Floyd.

Lobb wore a standard two-piece suit, the business-dress FBI look, which along with the close knee-to-knee seating was designed to unsettle and intimidate Floyd. The plan going in was that, in the event Floyd displayed any anger, it would be directed towards Lobb. Furr, by contrast, would sit in the back next to the table. He would appear more relaxed and casual in a sports coat and polo shirt. He had also grown a long, red-gray beard, following a belief that a well-kept beard improved credibility. Lobb would handle most of the questioning, while Furr would observe and, when necessary, interject, especially if things got heated.

It was around 8:30 a.m. when they heard the shackles outside in the hallway. When the door opened, a corrections officer slowly led Franklin Floyd into the room. Now seventy-two, he was balding and thin. For the past eleven years he had spent twenty-three hours a day in his jail cell—the by-product of a death row conviction—and it had taken its toll. What was left of his gray hair was unkempt, and his face was wrinkled and devoid of color. He appeared sickly. He wore an orange prison jumpsuit with a gray sweatshirt underneath. An iron chain was wrapped around his thin waist, while leg irons were clamped around his ankles.

The corrections officer directed Floyd towards a chair and then left the room. Floyd appeared bewildered. He had been notified just minutes earlier that he had visitors. He rarely had visitors, only lawyers handling the appeal of his death sentence in the Cheryl Commesso case, so he figured they were back. But he didn't recognize these two men and immediately thought he'd been assigned new attorneys.

"I'm appealing the Commesso case, you know," said Floyd. "I didn't kill Commesso."

In his hands were papers that he said were important to his appeal. After he carried on for a few minutes, Lobb motioned for him to stop talking and pulled out his identification.

"Mr. Floyd, we can't really do anything for you on the Commesso case," he said. "That's not what we're here for. We're not attorneys."

"Well, then, why the fuck you here?" said Floyd, his voice raised.

"I'm Special Agent Lobb from the FBI. This is Nate. We're here to talk about the Michael Hughes case."

Floyd paused, clearly annoyed with the sudden turn and the subject matter.

"Michael Hughes!" he yelled. "What the fuck do you want to talk about, how I got screwed?"

"Tell me," said Lobb, directing him to sit down and then sitting next to him.

The close proximity startled Floyd, but it didn't stop him from venting about his "unjust" conviction and how he'd be a free man if it weren't for FBI agent Joe Fitzpatrick and Mark Yancey, the assistant U.S. attorney in Oklahoma City who had prosecuted Floyd along with Ed Kumiega in 1995.

"Do you realize the case I have for my appeal?" he argued. "This should have been thrown out long ago!"

Floyd's anger towards Fitzpatrick was deep, and he spoke about how Fitzpatrick and Yancey had led a government conspiracy to put him in prison.

"I was fucked. You know that," said Floyd. "I mean, let me tell you, I had a lot of friends who were in law enforcement, and I have tremendous respect for the FBI. But that guy Joe Fitzpatrick, he was nothing but a low-down motherfucker who did everything he could to pin this on me. And Yancey, he's from Florida, and he helped the fucking cops that set those pictures up. I know that. I can't tell you how, but that's part of my appeal."

The agents knew that Floyd was talking about the photos that he taped to the undercarriage of the pickup truck he stole after kidnapping Michael and his principal in 1994. The truck was eventually sold to the mechanic in Kansas who discovered the large envelope taped underneath.

But Lobb remained quiet, staying on script by letting Floyd ramble. Furr took notes. After about an hour of Floyd ranting his grievances and spewing story after story about his life and his innocence in the Commesso murder, Lobb thought it was finally time to interject.

"I want to ask you something, Mr. Floyd. Are you familiar with the book *A Beautiful Child*?" Floyd's sickly white face turned red.

"That fucking book!" he screamed. "That writer, Birkbeck, he's another fucking faggot! Ninety percent of that book is false. It's all bullshit, written just to make Fitzpatrick and Yancey and all those motherfuckers famous! I know this, I'm telling you. I know this!"

Floyd became unhinged, intermixing four-letter words with racist and homophobic slurs.

"I was in the business of making them all famous!" he yelled.

Lobb saw an opening. One of the early strategies discussed with Furr focused on trying to develop a rapport with Floyd. Lobb had to find *something* the two of them could talk about to engage Floyd, and he used his hatred towards the book and its author.

"OK, if only 10 percent of the book is right, tell us which parts?" said Lobb.

"Which parts?" said Floyd. "Don't you understand? That book, that writer, it was all part of a plan to lock me up! I'm not guilty of anything. They all worked together!"

"OK," said Lobb, still sitting knee-to-knee with Floyd. "Everybody else has told your story for you. I'm interested in Michael. You're a clever guy. You tell me what happened. You tell the story. I'm not Matt Birkbeck, Joe Fitzpatrick, or Mark Yancey, OK? I'm interested in you, in what you have to say."

Floyd bit.

He started by talking about his early life at the Georgia Baptist Children's Home in Hapeville. He could barely walk when he arrived with his four older siblings, but as the years passed they were filled with abuse, heartache and rebellion. Floyd then moved on to his criminal exploits as a young man. There was the time, he said, when he broke into a Sears store in Los Angeles in 1960 and tried to steal a gun, only to get into a shootout with the police that left him wounded with a bullet in his gut. He robbed a bank in Ohio in 1962 and was caught and sentenced to fifteen years in prison. Shortly after, he explained, he tried to escape by hot-wiring a fire truck with two other inmates, but they crashed the vehicle and were captured. Floyd was sent to the maximum-security federal prison in Lewisburg, Pennsylvania.

Floyd was proud of his criminal accomplishments, especially his ability as a free man to navigate the criminal justice system. Wherever he had lived, Floyd said, he had made a point of befriending local police officers and cultivating relationships that, at times, proved handy. He eventually took Lobb and Furr to the late 1970s, when he worked as a painter, but Lobb wanted him to focus on the early part of the decade, when after his release from prison in 1973 he violated his parole by attacking a woman at a gas station. The woman was in a car, and her screams forced Floyd to flee. Floyd again began to talk about the late 1970s, but Lobb stopped him. As the lead interviewer, he did most of the talking, elevating his voice when Floyd raised his and speaking evenly when Floyd was calm. Lobb walked him back to 1974.

"Who was Sharon Marshall?" he asked.

Floyd paused, seemingly unwilling to address the question. There was a knock on the door, and in walked the corrections officer. It was now 11:30 a.m. and Floyd had to report for a prisoner head count and lunch. He was led away, and Lobb and Furr waited a few minutes before leaving the prison for a quick lunch at a Pizza Hut. But the food became cold as they talked about the interview.

Lobb was still pumped. Picking at his food, he expressed concern to Furr about his ability to keep Floyd on track and ultimately get him to spill his secrets.

For his part, Furr had followed his prescribed role by remaining calm and cool and focused on Floyd's answers. Now, Lobb wanted to hear the opinion of the interrogation expert on how well, or poorly, he had handled Floyd.

"What do I need to change?" asked Lobb.

"Floyd likes to take people down rabbit holes. I'd stop that," said Furr. "I think we can be a little more forceful in where we want the discussion to go. We want to talk about Sharon, but also who killed her and what happened to Michael. Talking about Sharon might be easier, the least intrusive for him instead of two murders. So let's see if he'll engage."

The agents had planned to remain in Florida four days. The expectation was that if Floyd was going to break, it would be during one of the sessions later in the week. The questioning on this first day was intended to lay the foundation for what they hoped would be a confession later. And if not during this trip to Florida, then during a second visit.

Game plan in hand, the pair headed back to the prison. Floyd was brought in around 1:00 p.m. He remained shackled around his midsection and ankles, but he was noticeably calmer and quieter. Furr sat in the back again while Lobb took his position in the chair next to Floyd. He didn't waste any time.

"So, who was Sharon Marshall? Did you kill her, and what happened to Michael?"

Floyd became agitated again.

"Do you have to sit so close to me?" he said to Lobb, who ignored the question.

Floyd then looked over to Furr, who was writing notes. Furr had intentionally avoided eye contact with Floyd during the morning, and he wasn't about to start now.

"Hey, look at me," instructed Lobb.

Floyd was annoyed. He pointed to Furr. "What the hell is he doing? He's just sitting there writing."

"Don't worry about him," said Lobb. "Look at me. Let's go back to 1973. You go on the lam. Where did you go?"

Floyd didn't want to go there. Instead, he spent two hours telling several stories, including one about getting into the military, but the agents knew they were all lies. Lobb would respond with a specific question, but Floyd would deflect it, answering with something like "Oh, I know where you got that from, my sister Dorothy. Well, let me tell you about her ...," and then he would spend a half hour complaining about his sister.

Lobb also brought up David Dial, whom Floyd had befriended when both were at the Reidsville prison, in Georgia. A convicted child molester, Floyd had been routinely raped and beaten at the prison. It was Dial, a big man, who eventually took it upon himself to protect Floyd. The men remained friends after each was released, but Floyd didn't want to talk about Dial. Just bringing up Dial's name made him angry.

Lobb calmed him down and brought Floyd back to where he wanted him, to 1973, and Floyd began telling another tale, this one about how he became a bus driver in North Carolina.

"I looked good in my uniform. I was the best bus driver around," he said proudly.

Just another bullshit story, thought Lobb, who was about to put his hand up to change the conversation when he looked at Furr, who signaled to let Floyd continue with this story and see where this went. Furr noticed that, unlike Floyd's previous stories when he became emotional and his voice elevated, he was now speaking calmly and staring straight ahead, apparently focused on actual details.

"I was working and stopped at a truck stop diner, where I met a woman who had lost her three kids."

"What was her name?" asked Lobb.

"It was Sandra Brandenburg."

"What was your name?"

"Brandon Cleo Williams."

It was a new name, an alias the agents had not heard before.

"She was a prostitute," said Floyd. "She was down on her luck. She had three kids but lost them to the state. We got to know each other, and being a good Christian man, I told her I would marry her and help her get her kids back."

"Who were these kids?" said Lobb.

"The oldest was named Suzanne, Suzanne Sevakis."

"Who is she?"

"That's your Sharon Marshall," said Floyd.

"Really?" said Lobb. "Where was she born?"

"Livonia, Michigan," said Floyd, without hesitation.

Lobb thought it was yet another bullshit story. He remembered Floyd had once said that another woman, a prostitute named Linda Williams, was Sharon's mother. But Floyd had admitted that was a lie, just another of the yarns he fed to law enforcement to buy himself time. He didn't explain what time he was buying.

Still calm and staring straight ahead, Floyd told how he had married Sandra Brandenburg in 1974 and then traveled with her and her three daughters to live with her family in Pennsylvania, near Reading. The girls were young, with Suzanne around five years old and the others maybe three and two, he said.

They remained in Pennsylvania for a few months before moving to Saint Charles, Missouri. From there, they traveled to Dallas. It was in Texas, said Floyd, that his new wife began an affair with someone at a church they attended, and she also began turning tricks, which she had done before.

"She was arrested," said Floyd.

"What for?" asked Lobb.

"A hot-check violation," said Floyd. "There was a warrant for her arrest for writing a bounced check in North Carolina."

"How much was the check?" said Lobb.

"I don't know, I think for one dollar," said Floyd.

He couldn't explain how the police in Texas happened to find Sandra. It could have been for prostitution, he said. But she was taken into custody and jailed for a month, leaving her three daughters with him.

"I knew this wasn't going to work out," said Floyd. "She would never stop being a prostitute. And those girls were a handful, especially the little ones. I knew I couldn't take care of three little girls."

So, Floyd said, he decided he would leave. But the oldest daughter, Suzanne, wanted to go with him. Of the three girls, he was closest with Suzanne.

So he said he placed the two younger girls with a children's Baptist home in Dallas and took off with Suzanne.

"I saved her," said Floyd.

"Who did you save?" said Lobb.

"Suzanne."

Floyd said he initially took her to Washington State, where he got a job picking apples, and then in August 1975 to Oklahoma City, where, under the name Trenton Davis, he enrolled his "daughter," Suzanne Davis, in public school.

The interview with Floyd ended around 4:00 p.m., and as soon as the two agents got into their rental car, Furr was on his cell phone with the FBI's Charlotte, North Carolina, field office. Floyd's story about meeting a woman with three children in North Carolina could be something of substance, they thought, or just another of Floyd's elaborate lies. To be sure, Furr called an agent he knew in Charlotte and he asked if he could search for a marriage certificate for a Brandon Cleo Williams and Sandra Brandenburg.

"Yes, it's W-i-l-l-i-a-m-s," said Furr, spelling out the name. "OK, we'll be in the car for a while, so I'll be waiting for your call."

He then dialed another number, this one for Tom Plantz, an FBI agent assigned to Lansing, Michigan, which was a satellite of the Detroit field office. Furr said he was looking for a birth certificate for a Suzanne Sevakis, born in 1969 in Livonia, a Detroit suburb. Plantz, who was a forensic artist for the bureau there, had an idea. He could put Furr in touch with a Sarah Krebs, a Michigan State Police trooper who headed the state police missing persons unit. Plantz called Krebs at her home that evening, gave her the briefest of outlines, and asked her to call Furr, which she did immediately.

Furr began to tell Krebs what he was doing in Florida, about the unidentified girl at the center of the mystery, and that he was looking for a birth certificate. She suddenly stopped him.

"Wait a minute," she said. "You're talking about Franklin Floyd! You're not going to believe it, but I just read a book about that case."

Furr was floored. As part of her job, Krebs was also the state expert on historical child crimes and often read up on national cases. Just six months earlier, she had read *A Beautiful Child*.

"I know this case," she said in her distinct Yooper, or Upper Peninsula, Michigan, accent. "Let me work on it."

Less than fifteen minutes later, Furr's phone rang. It was his FBI agent friend in North Carolina. He had found a 1974 marriage certificate for a Sandra Brandenburg and Brandon Cleo Williams.

"Holy shit," said Furr. "Floyd was telling the truth!"

Chapter 8:
Day Two

Scott Lobb and Nate Furr had just left the Union Correctional Institution the following morning, having finished a frustrating first session of the day with Franklin Floyd, when Furr's cell phone buzzed, alerting him to a new email.

It was from Michigan State Police trooper Sarah Krebs, and her message was simple, yet startling.

"You have a new best friend! Call me."

Furr turned to Lobb, who was driving.

"She got it!" said Furr. "She got the birth certificate!"

The two FBI agents, still giddy over confirming Floyd's story about marrying Sandra Brandenburg in North Carolina in 1974, were now beside themselves after hearing that, yes, Suzanne Sevakis was their Sharon Marshall.

Krebs, who, after speaking to Furr the night before, had reached out that morning to the Michigan Vital Records office, asking for a check on a birth certificate for a Suzanne Sevakis, born in Livonia around 1969.

The confirmation came quickly, but Krebs's email to Furr to call her didn't reach him until lunchtime. Neither Furr nor Lobb had their cell phones at the time. They were required to give them up upon entering the prison that morning for their second day of interviews with Franklin Floyd.

Furr immediately called Krebs, who said she was still awaiting a copy of the actual document, but had been told that the girl known as Sharon Marshall, and nearly a dozen other names, was born Suzanne Marie Sevakis at 6:43 p.m. on September 6, 1969 at Saint Mary Hospital in Livonia, Michigan. She was the daughter of a Sandra Francis Chipman, age nineteen, and Clifford Ray Sevakis, twenty. Krebs said there was also a birth certificate for another daughter, Allison, who was born in 1970.

If either Sandra or Clifford was still alive, a simple DNA test would confirm Sharon's real identity.

Within minutes after the call, Krebs had a copy of the birth certificate, and she forwarded it to Furr.

Now Furr and Lobb had the paperwork in hand and Lobb could go into the second afternoon session with Floyd knowing what the truth looked like. And the paperwork couldn't have come sooner, given that the morning session had been a disaster.

Floyd had already been inside the interview room waiting when they arrived, around 8:15 a.m. The agents immediately realized they had made a mistake in telling him they'd be back the next morning. To their surprise, Floyd, still chained, had rearranged the furniture, moving it back to its original setting.

"You think I don't know what you're doin'?" said Floyd. "Your interviewing techniques weren't working. I'd been trained as good as you were."

Instead of sitting next to Floyd, Lobb now had to sit across from him, separated by the table. From there it was all downhill. Floyd was back to his old self, resisting nearly every question posed by Lobb, who tried but failed to get Floyd to pick up where they'd left off on the timeline. When Floyd didn't respond, Lobb jumped ahead several years, which infuriated Floyd.

"Fuck you, you faggot" was among the nicer things Floyd said amid the torrent of curses and slurs he hurled at Lobb.

Floyd would alternately cry and snot up and then scream at the agents, especially Lobb. Floyd was spitting fire—a spectacle that, with the change of seating, could be seen outside in the hallway through the big window. Floyd didn't care. He had given the agents something he had never divulged before, Sharon's true identity. And after twelve years on death row, he wanted something back. By midmorning, he demanded to be moved to a federal prison facility.

"We can't do that," said Lobb.

"Of course you can!" screamed Floyd. "You're fucking federal agents! You have the power. I was a police officer. I painted FBI agents' houses. I know how this works. If you're in charge, then you can sure as shit make this happen!"

They knew that Floyd had never been a police officer, one of several occupations Floyd falsely claimed that morning.

"We can't do that," said Lobb.

"Motherfuckers!" screamed Floyd.

He threatened to end the discussions and go back to his cell. The agents let him rant until 11:30, when he had to leave for the prison head count and lunch.

When they returned that afternoon, with the birth certificate in hand, they told Floyd they believed him. He had been truthful. But

Floyd's disposition remained as cold and angry as it had been throughout the morning. He screamed and cursed whenever he felt that Lobb, sitting across from Floyd, had violated his "personal space." Whatever trust they may have gained from the first day interviews had been lost. Fearing a total emotional meltdown, Furr decided it was time for him to step in and try something different.

Up until now he was just some guy named Nate. So he pulled out his identification and said he was Special Agent Nate Furr. Floyd reached over with his shackled hands to touch the badge.

"You don't know how much I respect this," said Floyd. "You know, I met Herbert Hoover!"

"Really?" said Furr, trying to convince Floyd he believed him.

"I went on a trip in high school and I met Mr. Hoover. It was a humbling experience," he said.

Furr tried to mimic a Southern drawl and spoke slowly and softly, which he hoped would be more comforting and familiar for Floyd compared with Lobb's more assertive approach. The change in strategy appeared to work as Floyd calmed down and began to talk about Sharon.

"I took care of her, I fed her, I clothed her, I picked out her schools. She was smart and needed the right kind of schools to excel. I knew that," he said.

Furr took him ahead, to Sharon's last days in Tulsa and the night she died in Oklahoma City.

Floyd explained that he drove Sharon, then known as Tonya, to Oklahoma City for an appointment with a gynecologist. He said he learned later that a car had hit her and that the police found red paint chips on the road.

"What did you think of the accident report and of the investigation?" said Furr, working to establish some kind of connection with Floyd.

"I will tell you man to man that was the best investigation I'd ever seen," said Floyd.

Of course, Lobb and Furr knew he was lying. There was very little investigative work and just the few pages from the accident report. They also knew that Floyd had owned a red truck but sold it to a friend about a month before Sharon's death The police theory was that Floyd intentionally sold the vehicle to a trusted friend knowing the same vehicle would be used later to strike Sharon, whose death was eventually ruled a homicide.

Floyd didn't want to talk anymore about Sharon's death. The agents asked for his thoughts on allegations by others that he had killed her, but he wasn't having any of it. He was emotional, but believing he would never reveal what really happened that night, the two agents decided it was time to end the interview.

When they returned to their hotel, they held a conference call with an FBI analyst back in Oklahoma City. A quick check on Facebook led them to Sandra Brandenburg. She was alive and living in Virginia Beach, Virginia. And trooper Krebs in Michigan had run a license check for a Cliff Sevakis. He was also alive and living near Detroit.

Lobb and Furr said they'd visit them both, but first they had to finish up with Floyd.

Day three began as day two had ended, with Floyd combative and uncooperative.

The seating arrangements remained as they were the day before, with Furr in the corner and Lobb sitting across the table from Floyd. For his part, Floyd wouldn't let the two agents get a word in for nearly an hour as he spewed venom, mostly towards Lobb again.

Lobb finally tried to start a conversation about Sharon, asking again about her death and about their movements throughout the country, but Floyd wouldn't have it.

So Furr again interceded and framed questions around what he had learned from *A Beautiful Child*. He started by complimenting Floyd on his parenting skills. He and Lobb knew Floyd was a monster, but if saying something nice would calm him, then so be it. Drawing from the book, they tried to direct the conversation around his history with Sharon.

"You know, she was smart and excelled in school. She couldn't have done that if you hadn't raised her to study," said Lobb.

Floyd perked up. "I raised her right," he said proudly. "I always tried to steer her straight."

Floyd claimed credit for her stellar grades, her work with the Air Force ROTC, and her scholarship to Georgia Tech.

"I was always looking to get her into the best schools, I can tell you that!" he beamed.

From Sharon's schoolwork they shifted to her friends, and the mention of Jennifer Fisher drew yet another outburst, which was likely born of Jennifer's testimony against Floyd at the 1995 kidnapping trial in Oklahoma City.

So the agents quickly shifted gears again and went back to Sharon, spending the better part of the third afternoon session talking about her accomplishments. As the interview neared its end, Lobb asked Floyd about Sharon's first pregnancy, the one in high school that forced her to give up her college scholarship.

"What happened to that baby?" said Lobb.

Floyd had been speaking in glowing terms of Sharon. He fed off her success and took pride in her accomplishments. But mentioning her pregnancy or her work as a nude dancer drew out his violent, dark side, something the agents had seen all too often over their three days with him.

"She got pregnant. Ruined her life! We went to Texas and she gave up the baby for adoption to doctors," he said, his voice rising. "Why do you care about that fucking whore!"

It was time to go, and Lobb and Furr welcomed the corrections officer who arrived to take Floyd back to his cell. They were done talking about Sharon Marshall. They had gotten Floyd to reveal her identity, ending what had been a decades-long mystery. Now, it was time to solve another secret: what happened to Michael Hughes.

That would be the subject for day four with Franklin Floyd. The agents weren't sure if the bureau would send them back to Florida, and they believed they were running out of time.

So, after sitting down to begin the fourth and final day of interviews, Lobb began immediately with September 12, 1994, the day Michael was kidnapped. Floyd explained that he was Michael's father and he tried to gain legal custody of the boy, but his claim to paternity was refuted by a DNA test and the courts. So he decided to take matters into his own hands.

"Michael was my boy," said Floyd. "You have to understand a father's love for his child. He belonged with me."

Floyd said he spent several weeks canvassing Michael's school and the home of his foster parents, Ernest and Merle Bean. Floyd didn't like Ernest Bean, whom he falsely accused of sexually assaulting Michael. He apparently did like Merle Bean, whom he only identified as "Mama."

He then told the story of how he entered the principal's office, pulled out a gun, and walked the principal at gunpoint to the door to Michael's classroom. After Michael was pulled from the class, he left with the boy and the principal in the principal's pickup truck, tied the principal to a tree a couple of miles away, and then took off. He said they eventually stopped in nearby Del City to buy some toys for Michael.

"Oh, it was great," said Floyd. "We were having the best time. I was having so much fun!"

"What kind of toys did you get him?" said Furr.

"Oh, you know, some knickknacks. A little ball with the paddle, stuff like that," said Floyd.

But Michael was upset and began asking for his mama, Merle Bean.

"That was sad to me because she was his real mama, not Sharon. I felt a little upset," he said.

Floyd then said he drove toward the Oklahoma-Texas state line towards Dallas.

"Tell me about that drive," said Furr.

"We just drove. Nothin' to tell," said Floyd.

He was withdrawing again. The agents had brought along a book of photos to use if they had to help Floyd recall certain people or events. Lobb dipped into the book and pulled out a photo of Michael and then leaned across the table to show to Floyd, who became irate.

"Why the fuck do you give a shit about this kid. He's dead," said Floyd, whose answer startled the agents.

"So he's dead?" said Lobb.

"I didn't say that," said Floyd, who paused to regain his composure. "I meant the guy who helped me is dead."

Floyd said he met someone at the Crossroads shopping mall at the intersection of two interstates, I-240 and I-35, in south Oklahoma City. He initially alluded to it being his old friend David Dial and that he had handed off the boy, who he claimed was now working for the government.

The agents wouldn't have any of that story.

"You're a smart man, but I'm not sure you know how DNA and Codis works," said Furr. "If Michael worked for the government, we'd have his DNA and we'd have run it through Codis and there would have been a hit, but we don't."

Furr was lying to Floyd, but time was running out.

"Oh," said Floyd, changing up his story again. "He's with a secret organization."

"So you dropped him off? Tell me about your trip down to Texas," said Furr, who pulled out a blank sheet of paper. "You know every story has a prologue and epilogue and inside is what really happened."

"Yeah," said Floyd. "That's the omission."

Furr was shocked that Floyd would know that expression, but he reached down and drew a circle anyway.

"This is what I want. This is Crossroads Mall at I-240 and I-35 in Oklahoma, and this is the Wonder Bread store in Dallas where you left the truck, and this is what I need," said Furr, pointing to the empty middle. "And no matter where you go, I'm going to keep walking back to it."

"Nate, I'm not mad at you, but I'm not going to tell you," said Floyd. "Let's just agree I'm not going to tell you."

"I need to know what's in the middle," said Furr.

"I'm just not going to go there," said Floyd. "I like you, but I can't tell you why."

The agents had walked Floyd to the point of admitting that Michael was dead, but they couldn't get him to go any further. Time had run out. The four days of interviews were over, and they left the prison disappointed.

They also knew they had more work to do.

Chapter 9:
Meeting the Parents

When Scott Lobb and Nate Furr returned to Oklahoma City following their interviews with Franklin Floyd, the first thing they did was call Joe Fitzpatrick and ask if he would come to the bureau office as soon as possible for a debriefing.

We have some news, Lobb told him.

Fitzpatrick hurried over and, seated alongside the agents' supervisor, Neil Hunt, he heard the words he never thought he'd hear in his lifetime: Sharon Marshall has been identified.

Lobb said her real name was Suzanne Marie Sevakis and that Floyd had confessed on their first day there. His story had thus far checked out.

Fitzpatrick was dumbstruck. So many years had passed that it didn't seem possible. He was so taken aback, he initially didn't believe them. But Furr showed Fitzpatrick her birth certificate and a marriage certificate for Sandra Brandenburg and one Brandon Cleo Williams, a.k.a. Franklin Delano Floyd.

"I gotta tell you, I'm in shock," said Fitzpatrick.

He knew Floyd well and had warned Lobb and Furr that their trip to meet with him in Florida would likely be a waste of time. But there it was, Sharon's real name. Confirmed.

"I thought I'd go to my grave never knowing who she was," said Fitzpatrick. He then looked directly at Lobb and Furr.

"Thank you," he said, expressing gratitude and appreciation for their work.

He then had a request.

"Can I tell Matt Birkbeck?"

Lobb and Furr paused for a second or two.

"Yes," said Lobb. "But not right now. We're hoping to go back to Florida again and see if we can get a confession about Michael and want to keep things quiet until we do. We don't want him or anyone else to put something out. That OK?"

Fitzpatrick replied that he trusted me enough to know I wouldn't leak any information, but if the agents wanted to keep things quiet for now, then why not. They deserved it.

Besides, they still had interviews immediately ahead.

The plan was for them to visit with Sandra Brandenburg, whom they believed they had found in Newport News, Virginia. But first they'd fly to Detroit, where they were going to sit down with Sharon's biological father, Cliff Sevakis.

Michigan State Police sergeant Sarah Krebs was counting down the minutes to when Scott Lobb and Nate Furr's early morning flight from Oklahoma City would arrive at Detroit Metropolitan Airport.

Krebs was there to meet the agents and drive them north to meet with Cliff Sevakis. Unsure of Cliff's role in the disappearance of his daughter, and fearful that he might run if he got advance notice, the visit and subsequent interview was to be a surprise. Her plan was to simply drive up to his front door with the FBI agents in tow and knock.

But as she waited in her blue and gray uniform for the agents to deplane, Krebs was excited. As with so many other law enforcement officials who'd read the tragic details of Sharon's life, the case was now personal. Krebs even thought there could be some karma at play, since she had just read the book a few months earlier and now have a key role to play.

So after her introduction to the agents, the three of them drove north to neighboring Rochester and stopped in front of a well-kept home, where Krebs led the two agents to the front door and delivered a cold, hard knock.

A woman answered, and Krebs identified herself, as did Lobb and Furr, with all showing their identification. Krebs asked if they could speak to a Clifford Sevakis. The woman identified herself as his wife and said her husband was inside. She led them into the living room and a man in his sixties of medium height and weight emerged from an adjoining room, where he had been packing. He and his wife were moving to Seattle to be near their two grown children.

Following brief introductions, Lobb and Furr asked Cliff to sit down, and they got right to it.

"Do you have a child from a previous relationship?" said Lobb.

Cliff appeared shocked by the question as Lobb went through some of Cliff's history. He stated that he'd had a daughter in 1969 with a woman named Sandra, that they married soon after and eventually divorced.

"Yes," said Cliff. "I did have a daughter. Her name was Suzanne."

Cliff explained that he and Sandra had been high school sweethearts and got married in 1968, soon after graduation. He attended college for a semester, dropped out, and was drafted into the army. While in basic training, he said, he learned that Sandra was pregnant. He was in Vietnam when she gave birth, on September 6 1969, and saw his daughter for the first time six months later in Hawaii. But the reunion wasn't a happy affair. Sandra asked for a divorce. Cliff said he was surprised and asked her to reconsider. Sandra agreed.

But a few months later Cliff received a letter from his father saying that his wife was having an affair with a man, Dennis Brandenburg, and that he should get home. Cliff was just a kid himself, only nineteen years old. When he arrived back in Michigan on a three-week leave, Sandra admitted that she was in love with another man and added that she was pregnant with that man's child. Cliff filed for divorce. That second baby, Allison, was born in 1970, before the divorce was completed. Hence, her last name on the birth certificate was also Sevakis.

Cliff was discharged from the army in 1971, but Sandra had moved to North Carolina by then, where she gave birth to yet another daughter, Amy. Cliff drove down with a friend to visit Suzanne in 1972. He didn't know it would be the last time he would see her.

A year later, Cliff received a letter from a social services office in North Carolina. Sandra had lost custody of her three daughters and, since they were close would he want to take them all? But then came another letter saying Sandra met another man and was about to get married again. Her soon-to-be husband, Brandon Cleo Williams, wanted to adopt her three daughters, and would Cliff be willing, Sandra asked, to give up his parental rights?

Cliff was barely into his twenties, didn't have a job, and thought a married man would be better equipped to raise his daughter, along with the other two. Not wanting to separate the three little girls, Cliff said, he agreed.

"That was the last time I ever heard about Sandra or Suzanne," he said.

Furr pulled out several photos of Sharon that were among the one hundred or so that had been in police custody and asked Cliff if he recognized her.

"Can that be your daughter?" Furr asked.

Maybe, Cliff said. He then listened intently as Lobb and Furr began to tell a story about a young woman named Tonya Hughes, who was killed in Oklahoma City in 1990. She had a little boy, Michael, they said, who was later kidnapped from his school and was never seen again.

"The girl had lived with a man, Franklin Floyd, and they had shown up in Oklahoma City in 1975 when she was a little girl. Her name was Suzanne Davis," said Furr.

Cliff tried his best to process what he was hearing. Initially, it didn't make any sense. But then came the sudden realization that something awful had occurred, and the anguish settled in.

"That's my daughter?"

"We believe so," said Lobb.

Cliff was devastated. The two agents and Krebs were sympathetic towards him, having dredged up his distant, painful past. It was a gut punch.

"We'd like to take a swab from you for a DNA test to confirm she is your daughter Suzanne," said Lobb.

Sickened by the story he'd just heard, Cliff agreed.

After leaving Cliff, Krebs drove the agents back to the airport, where they boarded a flight for Norfolk, Virginia. From Norfolk, they drove across the bay to Newport News and pulled into a large trailer park. They had a name, Sandra Brandenburg, and an address, but they weren't sure they had the right Sandra Brandenburg. Navigating the narrow streets, they finally stopped in front of a tiny trailer. The visit was a surprise. Whoever was inside certainly wouldn't be expecting two FBI agents to knock on their door. A woman who appeared to be in her forties answered. She was startled when they identified themselves, but, yes, she said, a Sandra Brandenburg did live there.

"She's my mom," said the woman, who said her name was Dorothy.

She invited Lobb and Furr inside. A single air conditioner hummed, but didn't provide much relief given how hot it was inside the cluttered trailer. Dorothy introduced her mother, who was sitting in a wheelchair, the result, Dorothy said, of some unidentified illness that required the use of an oxygen tank that was next to her.

"Are you Sandra Brandenburg?" Lobb asked.

"Yes," she replied.

Lobb pulled out a photo from his shirt pocket.

"Do you know this man?"

Sandra didn't hesitate. "That's Brandon C. Williams," she said. "He stole my daughter."

"What was her name?" Furr asked.

"Suzanne. Suzanne Sevakis," said Sandra.

Sandra was thin and frail, her face old, worn, and tired. Lobb repeated the story told to Cliff about the tragic life of the little girl who first arrived in Oklahoma City in 1975 and died in Tulsa in 1990.

Dorothy began to cry, as did Sandra. But Furr didn't believe Sandra's tears. The two agents were hot and tired, having flown from Oklahoma to Detroit and then to Virginia the same day. They were also decidedly testy.

Furr was so angry with Sandra's admission that she knew the man in the photo, he wanted to jump at her and scream in her face, "Why weren't you searching for your daughter!"

Sandra never filed a police report or, from what the agents had gathered, demonstrated any effort to find her daughter. The only reference to her disappearance was a book, and without it, Furr knew, he and Lobb wouldn't have been there, inside this steaming, cluttered, tiny trailer, trying to solve a mystery.

Sandra should have done something, anything, to find her daughter. But she didn't, and the agents wanted to know why. It was a question they had asked themselves over and over since hearing Floyd's confession. Lobb was just as angry, but he wanted Sandra's DNA and didn't want to upset her so they could get the hell out of there and return home. But first they had a few more questions. Lobb took the high road, and the agents listened as Sandra told her story.

She had met Williams at a church near Charlotte. She was a single mother with three small daughters who were in state custody at the time. Sandra wouldn't say why, but it was clear she had issues. So when Brandon Cleo Williams showed interest in taking care of them all, and promised he would help her gain custody of her children, she jumped at the chance. Two weeks after meeting, they got married in front of a preacher.

"How was your marriage? Did you consummate it?" asked Lobb.

"He couldn't really have sex," Sandra said. "He had to hold me down. Sometimes he'd tie me down. I don't remember him ever having an orgasm without it being violent in some way."

"And how about the girls. How did he treat them?" asked Furr.

"He was close to Suzanne. She was more attached to him than the others," she said.

After living with her family in Pennsylvania for a brief time, Sandra said, they all moved to Saint Charles, Missouri. But Brandon Williams was always nervous, as if someone were always behind him, trailing him, stalking him.

"I didn't know much about him," Sandra said. "He said he had been in Florida and lived outside of Miami, working at jai alai, at a Caterpillar factory, and doing some handyman work. Then he went to New York before he came to Charlotte."

While in Saint Charles, Williams would rarely allow Sandra or the children to leave their home, even when he was gone for days on so-called "hunting" trips.

"He'd do that a lot," she said. "Just disappear."

They abruptly left Saint Charles after some neighbors, playing a joke on Floyd, moved his car from its parking spot to another one. He was spooked, and he moved the family to Dallas. It was there, Sandra said, where she was arrested for what she claimed was an old bad-check charge. Something about writing a $1.78 check to a 7-Eleven with no money in the account to buy milk for the kids. She spent a few weeks in a local jail, and when she was released, Brandon Cleo Williams was gone and had taken Suzanne with him, while the other two girls, Allison and Dorothy, were left at a local church.

And there was one more thing, she said, an infant son, Philip. But Sandra was vague about his fate. Lobb and Furr weren't sure they believed her.

They also had scant sympathy for her. She told her story with little emotion. Even the brief display of tears appeared insincere. But she agreed to give the agents her DNA. They returned the next day, spoke a little more, and dabbed the swab in her mouth and said good-bye.

They were glad to leave Sandra Brandenburg.

Chapter 10:

Sandra

S andra Chipman loved boys.

The oldest of three children born to a housewife and a field representative for General Motors, Sandra was a pretty high school student with an IQ that was off the charts and a disdain for after-school activities, especially sports. But she had other interests.

Her younger brother Jim would often say that "her extracurricular activities were boys."

Among the boys that Jim could remember she had dated more than fifty years ago at W.E. Groves High School in Beverly Hills, Michigan, were Bill the baseball player and Cliff, the amiable, soft-spoken boy from the neighborhood whom she would eventually marry.

Following graduation, Cliff dropped out of college after one semester and was soon drafted into the army and sent to Vietnam. Before he left, he and Sandra secretly wed. She still lived at home, and it wasn't long before her family noticed the bulging belly. Sandra first confessed to the pregnancy and then to having eloped with the soon-to-be father, Cliff Sevakis.

He was in Vietnam when she gave birth to a daughter, Suzanne, on September 6, 1969. The young family reunited six months later in Hawaii. It was supposed to be a happy time for Cliff, who saw and held his baby daughter for the first time. But Sandra, only nineteen, interrupted the reunion with a confession: she had begun an affair with another local boy, and she wanted a divorce. Cliff, only twenty, begged her to reconsider. But the discussion over their future was quickly pushed aside when Suzanne fell ill. She was rushed to the emergency room at the Tripler Army Medical Center in Honolulu. It took several days for her to recover, and by the time she was released, the family reunion was over. Sandra said she'd think about her decision, but it was too late. After she returned home, Cliff received a letter from his father telling him that Sandra had taken up with a Dennis Brandenburg. Cliff filed for divorce. But Sandra would give birth to another daughter in October 1970, Allison, before the divorce was finalized. So Allison bore Cliff's last name. Sandra would quickly give birth to a third daughter, Amy, and would follow her parents to Charlotte, North Carolina, where they lent her the money for a mobile home.

With three children to care for, Sandra turned to prostitution to supplement her welfare check, her family learned. By the time her fourth child, a boy, was born, she had begun to use drugs.

Sandra's brother Jim said years later that he remembered hearing about the drugs and the boy, who was born in a Charlotte hospital. But Sandra gave up her infant son, Phillip, in some sort of private adoption—no one really knew any details—and the state's child welfare office took custody of the girls with the intent of putting them up for adoption.

It was around that time that Sandra met Brandon Cleo Williams, the amiable truck driver. He promised to help get her children back and, just two weeks after meeting, they married. Soon after, in June 1974, the state returned the three children to Sandra's custody.

Sandra and her new husband and daughters would leave North Carolina for Reading, Pennsylvania, to be near Sandra's parents, who had moved there. Jim had just gone through his own divorce and was trying to piece his life together again, and he decided to go to Reading.

It was Christmas 1974 when Jim arrived. He recalls Brandon Williams as personable and easy to get along with, but with clear boundaries. He'd let you get close, but not too close. Jim figured Williams liked his privacy. He also saw that despite his sister's problems, his nieces appeared happy. Especially Suzanne, whom Jim remembers being a smart, happy child who was always trying to please.

Jim spent a few weeks in Pennsylvania before returning to Michigan. Soon after, in early 1975, he learned that Sandra, her new husband, and the children had also moved on, to Texas.

The next time Jim heard from Sandra, she said her husband had run off with Suzanne. They'd been living in Dallas when Sandra was arrested for writing a bad check. Brandon had dropped the two youngest girls with their church and took off with Suzanne.

The Chipman family tried to process what had happened and, knowing Sandra's ease with lying, they started to make their own calls. What they heard back from the police and church congregation was disturbing. It appeared that Sandra was still working as a prostitute and may have even been sent to jail on a solicitation charge. Even worse, she may have actually given Suzanne to Brandon and later traveled to Oklahoma to try to sell the other two children.

The family was confused and angry, and even more so when they learned that Sandra had never filed a police report.

Years would pass without much word or contact with Sandra, who would clam up whenever she was questioned about her missing daughter. By June 2014, she had given birth to seven children and was confined to a wheelchair and living in a trailer park in Newport News, Virginia.

That was around the time Jim received a call from FBI agent Scott Lobb, who was looking for a contact number or address for Sandra. Lobb at first wouldn't tell him why, but in a subsequent conversation the agent said Suzanne had been murdered and that if Jim was interested in learning what had happened, he should read a book about the case. Jim was devastated, but he and his wife, Cindy, immediately got a copy of *A Beautiful Child*. A long haul truck driver, he couldn't eat or sleep and for weeks as his thoughts were of the happy little girl he had known so long ago.

Chapter 11:
Killing Michael

By the end of August 2014, Scott Lobb and Nate Furr had decided it was time to go back to Florida and sit down again with Franklin Floyd.

This time, the topic would be Michael Hughes.

The six-year-old boy had last been seen in a pickup truck with Floyd on September 16, 1994, and the hope was that Floyd would follow his confession about Sharon's true identity with another admission as to the fate of the little boy.

Floyd had, over the years, told different stories about Michael—from having sent him to friends in South America to telling his sister Dorothy that he drowned the boy in a bathtub in Atlanta just days after kidnapping him.

As September neared, Lobb and Furr reduced their caseload to the point where they were able to get permission from their superiors to meet with Floyd again. They made arrangements with the prison to visit and flew to Florida on September 27, 2014. They spent that night and the next day in their hotel going over notes and strategizing over how they would make their approach to Floyd.

Having spent four days with him in May, they felt they knew him well. But they also knew he was slippery, duplicitous, and very smart. Getting him to confess to the murder of a child would be far more challenging.

September 29 was game day, and they entered the prison as they had before, following the strict security procedures to gain access to the death row area. They showed their credentials to a corrections officer, and their names were cross-referenced with a list of approved visitors. A gate was opened, they entered and waited for it to close, then a second gate allowed them to go before an X-ray machine and a magnetometer. A third gate led to a tiny room with just a button on the opposite wall. When it was pressed, a guard on the other side of the call box watching them on a monitor unlocked the gate and they entered a 200-foot-long, fenced walkway that took them to a final gate, which was the entrance to death row. They were placed in the same interview room as before, and within minutes a shackled Franklin Floyd was brought into the room.

"What the fuck are you guys doing back here?" said a startled Floyd. "I never thought I'd see you again. Don't you know I've been sick?"

The agents didn't know. Floyd had just been released from the prison hospital the day before after spending a week undergoing treatment for a pulmonary issue. Floyd looked gaunt and weak, and he was angry.

He complained that the guards had recently removed all of his case files from his cell, which he had obtained for his appeal of the Cheryl Commesso conviction. As he did before, he ranted uninterrupted for almost two hours, booming about his treatment at the prison, his innocence in the Commesso case, and every other perceived slight over the course of his life. Lethargic at first, Floyd finished his outburst with a flourish, cursing at the agents with a vengeance just as he had in May.

"Fuck you cocksuckers," he said. "You want to talk to me, you have to promise you're going to move me to a fed prison. You understand me? I don't want to be here."

Floyd's final outburst coincided with lunchtime, and he was led out of the room by a guard. When they resumed two hours later, Furr spoke immediately and ignored the request that he be moved.

"Listen, we need to get past all this. We came here to talk to you about Michael. We want you to focus on that. You understand?"

"Michael? What the fuck you want to talk about him for?"

"We want you to tell us what happened to him."

Floyd had a way of curling his lips into a crooked smile, especially when he believed he was in control, and he was doing it now.

"Well, I told you cocksuckers before that I gave him off. He's being cared for and raised by people I trust. I did tell you that, didn't I? So why keep asking me about him? I loved that boy with all my heart. I would never hurt him. I took care of him. I cleaned his diapers and fed him his milk. No one could love that boy the way I did."

The agents tried but couldn't get Floyd to focus on Michael, and the rest of the afternoon was torturous, much like the morning, with Floyd unwilling to engage in any kind of rational discussion. He spewed stream-of-consciousness drivel that couldn't be stopped. By 4:00 p.m., it was time for Floyd to go back to his cell, and Lobb and Furr lingered in the room trying to assess the damage.

"That was brutal," said Lobb. "I'm not sure where we go from here. I'm not even sure there is a place to go. Do we even come back tomorrow?"

"That was bad," Furr agreed. "But I'm wondering if he reacted that way because we pressed on Michael. The last time we spoke with him it was mostly about Sharon. But now ... I think, as bad as that was, we may have opened a door. I actually think we may be close. We have it in his head. So, yeah, we come back."

The following morning Lobb and Furr assumed the same positions in the room that they had marked out the day before: Furr in the rear, his back against the wall, and Lobb seated, directly across from Floyd.

But unlike the previous day they weren't going to allow Floyd to go off on a tangent or claim again that Michael was alive and living in some foreign country. They weren't going to go down *that* road again, especially since it was probably going to be their final interview with Floyd. Their last chance. So when he was brought in and placed in his chair, Lobb didn't waste any time.

"We are going to talk about Michael," he said in an even tone. "And I'm not hearing about you giving the child off. You understand?"

"I've been telling you the truth," said Floyd.

Lobb got up and walked out of the room.

"What got up his drawers?" said Floyd.

"He wants the truth, Floyd. We both do. And I think you do too," said Furr, who noticed Floyd was fidgeting. The screaming and complaints of the prior day had clearly morphed into what appeared to be Floyd entering "the confession phase," a law enforcement term for when someone who's committed a crime is contemplating a true confession.

Lobb walked back in and drew a death stare from Floyd.

"You need to get the fuck out," said Floyd, becoming more emotional.

"What is it?" Furr prodded. "C'mon, you can tell us. Did you kill him?"

Floyd stood up from his chair.

"He wanted to be back with his mother, Mama Bean, so I reached over—"

"Where, inside the truck?" said Furr.

"Yeah. I just reached over and choked him."

"Why?" said Furr. "Was he giggling? Did he shit himself? What did he do?"

"I don't really remember," said Floyd. "I got him toys and it wasn't far from there, by the lake."

"Is that the Stanley Draper Lake?" Furr asked, referring to a man-made lake in Oklahoma City.

"Yeah, it was over there. I threw him in a Dumpster. All his toys I bought him too. Then I drove down to the Wonder Bread store in Dallas," said Floyd. "Now, can you guys get me into a federal holding facility?"

The agents weren't buying it.

"No," Lobb cut in. "Not on a lie. We can't take that."

"But that's what fucking happened!" Floyd screamed.

"I believe you killed him, but not in that manner," said Furr.

"But let's talk about that," said Lobb. "You told us you killed him, and that's fine. I'm glad we got to that point. But we need to know how you did it."

He then tried to move the conversation forward, but Floyd wouldn't have it, and they tiptoed around what actually happened that day, with Lobb becoming increasingly frustrated, his voice rising in anger. After three hours, Floyd had had enough of Scott Lobb.

"Fuck you, I'm done," he said.

It was lunchtime, and Floyd was led out of the room by a guard. But before he cleared the door he turned back toward the agents with another crooked smile.

"I'll see you after lunch."

Lobb and Furr followed him out into the hallway.

"What's that about?" said Furr, of Floyd's good-bye.

Floyd could be heard yelling down the hall, drawing the attention of other inmates and guards. The two agents didn't respond. But when Floyd returned to the interview room Furr began the questioning and Floyd's raw anger, which had been directed towards Lobb, quickly shifted to Furr.

"You embarrassed me! I thought you were a good person," Floyd yelled.

"You're toying with us," said Furr. "You need to realize that this place, this prison, is where you are going to die and all these little things to keep us off pitch will never work. Scott and I are here for one purpose, and that is to have closure for Michael. Do you understand what I'm telling you?"

Floyd just stared at the agents, who were now sitting across from him side by side.

"I want you to know," said Lobb, "that we had a conversation with the U.S. attorney's office, and nobody is going to be prosecuted in this case even if we found a body. Which means you will not be charged. All we want to know is what happened."

Floyd fidgeted.

"You know, I had twenty thousand FBI agents on my tail, looking for me," he said. "So I'm driving, and Michael was upset."

"How upset?" said Furr.

"Very upset. Didn't you listen to me before when I told you he wanted Mama Bean?"

"You mean Merle Bean, his foster mother, right?" said Furr.

"Of course," Floyd said. "I don't think she did right by him. But when I had him he was brilliant. It was the Beans' fault. If he were alive today he'd be autistic."

"What do you mean by 'alive today'?" Furr asked. "So you're saying he's dead? Did you strangle him?"

Floyd stood up and, though shackled around the wrists and legs, turned around to face the back wall. Furr rose, walked around the table, and stood next to him.

"No, I didn't want him to attract attention. I figured they'd found the principal by then," said Floyd, referring to the school principal he had tied to a tree after taking Michael.

"When you took him, did you think you were saving him like you did with Sharon?" Furr asked.

Floyd began to sob, and Furr whispered into his ear, "C'mon, Floyd, just tell us. You want to. I *know* you do. Just *tell* us what happened."

"I just couldn't take it," said Floyd, still sobbing. "Michael kept screaming he wanted to go back."

"And?" said Furr.

Floyd didn't respond, so Lobb, still in his chair, moved in and slapped his hand down hard on the table.

"How did you kill him?" said Lobb, barely able to contain himself.

Floyd, still facing the wall, didn't respond. Lobb again slapped his hand on the table and demanded that Floyd tell him the truth.

Floyd wouldn't speak. Instead, he became even more irrational and cried uncontrollably. Furr tried to reassure him that everything would be OK once he confessed. Through all their interviews, and despite all of Floyd's previous outbursts, they'd never seen him as raw and exposed as this. Furr looked over to Lobb with a look that said, *We got him.*

"C'mon, Floyd, it's over. *Tell* us," whispered Furr.

Floyd looked up towards the ceiling and, turning his shackled hands palms upward, cried out, "Why, God, have you forsaken me?!"

There was a long pause, but nothing followed. Lobb, his face now red with anger, punched down hard on the table and roared, "*How did you kill him, dammit! Tell us now!*"

Floyd looked at Furr, who knew what was about to come. The emotion and tears were gone, replaced by a blank expression. Floyd then turned around, his vacant eyes staring directly at Lobb.

"I shot him twice in the back of the head to make it real quick," he said matter-of-factly.

All the screaming and crying that had filled the interview room most of the day was now replaced by an utter silence. Five seconds passed, then ten, then twenty. A guard outside the room peeked in through the glass to make sure everything was all right.

Scott Lobb's heart was racing, while Nate Furr stood stunned. Nearly twenty years to the day since Michael Hughes was kidnapped from his first-grade classroom, Franklin Floyd had finally confessed to murdering the boy.

Lobb composed himself and, trying to play down the revelation, asked Floyd in a calm, reassuring voice about the caliber of the gun he had used.

"Was it a thirty-two or three-eighty?"

Floyd slowly shuffled to the chair, his shackles clanging, and sat down. Furr walked over to his chair next to Lobb.

Floyd was spent, the emotions of the day having drained his will to dodge, lie, berate, and otherwise toy with the agents. That was all over, and the agents listened as Floyd relayed what happened that day. He expressed his love for Michael and how he tried to talk to him as a father while they drove south on I-35 towards the Texas border. But Michael, he said, just wouldn't stop crying and yelling. He had lived with the Beans for four years and had grown to love them dearly. He was part of their family, and his resistance didn't provide the reunion Floyd had hoped for. Floyd said he knew he'd be captured unless he did something to quiet Michael.

"You got some paper?" he said.

Floyd drew a map from Oklahoma City, down I-35 to the last exit before the Texas state line. He then drew a curve and then another curve that led to a dead end between two roads. It was a desolate area, he said, nothing but dirt, tumbleweeds, and oak and cypress trees.

"That's where I did it," he said. "I parked the truck and we walked over by some trees. I put him down and left him."

"You just left his body there?" said Lobb.

"Yeah," said Floyd. "I can't believe I told you that."

He said he got back into the truck and, before he hit the highway again, threw the gun out the window off a bridge crossing. When he arrived in Dallas, Floyd said, he left the truck at the Wonder Bread factory, dyed his hair, and boarded a bus for Atlanta. He cried most of the trip, Floyd said, and kept looking out behind the bus for police lights, believing the bus would be stopped at any moment. Several days later he had a nervous breakdown and admitted himself into a psychiatric facility.

Floyd agreed to sign a confession, all the while trying to convince the agents that he loved Michael.

"I'm not a horrible person," Floyd said.

Lobb and Furr disagreed with Floyd's self-assessment, but said nothing. Instead, they told Franklin Floyd good-bye, certain, in fact hopeful, that they'd never see him again. Despite all his lies over the years, they believed his story and his confession. No one previously had spent so much time with him, which helped the agents sense when he was lying and when he was telling the truth. Specifically, when Floyd dropped the swagger and emotion and was forced to focus on a particular topic, he would stare in either Lobb's or Furr's eyes as he spoke, much as he had when he confessed to killing Michael.

Now, the agents wanted to get back to their hotel and confirm it. Once there, they looked at a map on a computer and quickly found the exit Floyd had drawn off I-35. It was in Thackerville, a little town near the Texas border, and surrounded on three sides by the Red River, which served as the state line. They followed the directions on Floyd's map, and it led to a remote area with open space, trees, and a lake, as Floyd had said.

Yes, it appeared he had told the truth. But they wanted to see the area firsthand, so after returning to Oklahoma City that night, they drove down the next day to Thackerville, accompanied by an analysis and evidence collector, and followed Floyd's directions to what he said was the murder site. Floyd had talked about driving an old road, maybe Route 77, that led to a wooded area with a lot of vegetation, which is exactly what the agents found. Route 77 ran parallel to I-35.

"I'll be damned," said Lobb. "He described this area like no one else can. Something definitely happened here."

The search area was much wider than they had expected, and a complete exploration would require many more agents, including evidence specialists, spending days, even weeks, at the site. They would also need the state medical examiner, who had experience searching for buried remains, as well as anthropologists familiar with searching in and near a lake. With the weather turning colder, snow on the horizon, and the time needed to schedule, it would be months before they could conduct such a search.

But as they walked through the area, Furr noticed something that would not help their cause: animal tracks, many of them, throughout the area, and, perhaps worst of all, those of feral pigs.

"We got a problem," he said, pointing to one set of tracks.

Wild pigs roamed the area and ate most anything they could find, including small animals. Furr followed one pig trail, taking pictures along the way of the bones that littered the ground, making sure they weren't human.

"You know that a body the size of Michael's wouldn't last long out here," said Furr. "The best we can hope for would be the bullets or shell casings or any metal from his pants."

The agents realized the task of finding any remains of Michael Hughes would be near impossible.

They returned in March 2015 with twenty agents and spent two days searching the area, with teams digging through the surface but they found nothing. That summer, on August 3, the FBI announced it had closed the Michael Hughes case.

FBI agents Scott Lobb (left) and Nate Furr. Their prison interviews with Franklin Delano Floyd produced two shocking confessions, and solved two great mysteries.

Ashley Rodriguez of the National Center for Missing & Exploited Children. Given the Sharon Marshall case in 2011, she enlisted a variety of experts, and eventually the FBI.
(Photo courtesy of Ashley Rodriguez).

Cliff Sevakis and Sandra Chipman on their wedding day.
Still teenagers, they eloped and kept their marriage a secret.
(Photo courtesy of Cliff Sevakis).

Cliff Sevakis (above, below) Dau Tieng base camp, Vietnam, 1969.
(Photos courtesy of Cliff Sevakis).

Cliff with Suzanne during leave, 1970.
(Photo courtesy of Cliff Sevakis).

Cliff Sevakis during his visit with Suzanne (standing)
and sister Allison in North Carolina, circa 1972.
(Photo courtesy of Cliff Sevakis).

Suzanne (above, and below) in North Carolina in 1972.
(Photo courtesy of Cliff Sevakis).

Cliff holding Suzanne. The visit in North Carolina would be the last time he saw his daughter, or speak to Sandra (below). Sandra would later frustrate her family and the authorities by not revealing all she knew about Suzanne's disappearance.
(Photo courtesy of Cliff Sevakis).

Sharon's son Michael fishing with foster father Ernest Bean. He was never seen again
after Floyd kidnapped him from his first grade classroom in 1994.
In 2015, FBI agents search for his remains near the Oklahoma/Texas border.
(Photos courtesy of Merle Bean and FBI).

Part
THREE

Chapter 12:
Tumbleweeds and Crayons

Tumbleweeds and crayons. Those are the two lasting images that Allison Sevakis remembers about her older sister.

Allison was only three, maybe four, years old when Suzanne disappeared, so the memories are few and faint. But they are there, somewhere deep inside. One memory is of two of them running and laughing as a strong Texas wind whipped around them while tumbleweeds bounced softly by. Allison can also remember the crayons scattered on the floor. They were from a box of sixteen, and she and Suzanne were drawing in a notebook.

"I asked my mom then who bought me the pack of crayons, and she said it was Suzy's dad," says Allison. "But I don't remember Suzy after that."

The second of seven children born to Sandra from multiple fathers, Allison is the only one who remembers Suzanne. Another sister, Amy, was too young at the time, while the others weren't born yet.

Today, over forty years later, Allison can still see Suzanne. But she also has other memories, nightmares really.

Allison was born October 19, 1970, in Livonia, Michigan, in the same hospital as her sister the year before. Her mother, Sandra, was attending Michigan State, paying her way through school while turning tricks, Allison says. Sandra's divorce from Cliff Sevakis had yet to be finalized, so Allison inherited his last name even though Cliff wasn't her father. She remembers, as a teenager, asking her mother multiple times about Cliff, only to be told again and again that he had been killed in Vietnam.

Eventually, Sandra told Allison that a man named Dennis Brandenburg was her biological father. But Allison thought that was a lie, even though Brandenburg was seeing Sandra while Cliff was in Vietnam. To this day Allison, at age forty-seven, has no idea who her biological father is. And she's not really searching.

She also hasn't spoken to her mother in years. It was a decision born of pain that runs deep, the result of losing a sister, of being abandoned, and of the incomprehensibility of a mother who never searched for a missing daughter.

A mother herself, Allison heard only bits and pieces of the story of her lost sister, mostly from Sandra. But there was never a sit-down, drawn-out explanation. There would be a question from Allison and a quick answer from her mother, who'd then shut down completely.

"Leave it alone" is how Sandra would end it. That's how it remained until 2014, when Allison's uncle Jim Chipman told her about a book. The family had just learned about the FBI's interviews with Brandon C. Williams, who was really Franklin Floyd, and that he had raised Suzanne as his daughter until her murder in 1990.

Sandra wasn't offering any additional information, but Uncle Jim said he'd been told about *A Beautiful Child* and that Allison should read it too. It would be a painful read, he cautioned.

It was.

Allison finished the book in a day. Distraught, she called her mother, and the first question was an old one: *why didn't she search for Suzanne?* Sandra hung up the phone. As she had so many times before, Sandra didn't want to answer decades-old questions about why she never tried to find her daughter.

Allison decided that was enough. She stopped communicating with her mother and hasn't spoken to her or any of her siblings since. They didn't know Suzanne, and, unlike Allison, they all had over the years come to the defense of their mother.

"Whenever I asked her what happened, she'd say she was kidnapped," Allison recalls. "So my thought is, why didn't you do anything to get her? She'd just say that her dad took her and it was none of my business."

In trying to piece together what happened so many years ago, she has tried to focus on Brandon Cleo Williams, a.k.a. Franklin Floyd. He was the only father figure in Allison's life, appearing around the time that her mother gave birth to a son. The son's name was Philip, or maybe Stevie, says Allison. He was Sandra's fourth child and first boy. But as quickly as he arrived, he was gone.

"I remember in the Carolinas she had a little boy, and then one day she didn't have him. She was pregnant, had the baby, brought it home, and then gave it to somebody. We called him Stevie," she says. "My mom first told me he was dead, but when I was older, social services in North Carolina told me he was very much alive. So my mom said later it was a private adoption. All I know is we never saw him again."

It was around the same time that "Brandon" arrived, and Allison and her sisters now had a stepfather.

The family left North Carolina to live near Allison's grandparents in Reading, Pennsylvania. After a few months they moved again, to Missouri, before settling in Dallas.

What she remembers of her stepfather is a man who would often vanish for days at a time. He also developed a strong relationship with Suzanne.

"He played favorites with Suzy," says Allison. "I've always been combative. Suzy wasn't like that. She was smart. They favored each other."

Perhaps the one memory that remains seared into Allison's psyche is she and Amy sitting on the steps of a church in Dallas. Allison recalls that her mother had been gone a few days. At the time Allison didn't know she had been arrested and was serving a thirty-day sentence. She remembers Brandon rounding up the children and driving them to a church and herself sitting with Amy sitting on the front stairs while Brandon and Suzanne drove off, never to be seen again.

Eventually, the two girls were taken inside and later placed with child-welfare services. When Sandra was released from prison she had to petition the courts to get them back. She eventually did, but it wasn't long after that, Allison remembers, before she and Amy were taken to Oklahoma. That was where Sandra tried to sell her two remaining daughters.

"These weren't legal channels," Allison recalls. "My mom read an article in the paper about how there were groups that were buying kids from people who couldn't afford them. But I guess she couldn't sell us."

Sandra returned to Dallas and, desperate, took the girls to a local police station, where she announced that she didn't want them. The police, Allison says, weren't empathetic and told Sandra to leave, with her children.

With no other options, Sandra and the girls hitchhiked back to North Carolina. Allison says she remembers being enrolled in kindergarten, but life over the next few years was a blur, with new men entering and then quickly leaving Sandra's life. The result was the birth of three more children: Jonathan, Jeffrey, and Dorothy.

By age ten, Allison says, she had heard whispers that her mother was working as a prostitute. It wasn't long after that that she was sent to the Jackson-Feild Girls Home in Emporia, Virginia, which specialized in treating children who experienced severe abuse and neglect. She remained there until she was nineteen, rarely seeing her mother or siblings.

"My mom said she didn't want me. I think I saw her twice the whole time I was away," she says.

After leaving the girls home, Allison met a boy and got pregnant. Today she lives in Oregon, far away from her mother and her siblings.

"It's sad, but I'm better off. I wanted to look for Suzy when I got out of the girls home," she says. "I asked my mom for the only picture she had of Suzy, me, and Amy together. We were on Santa's lap. That's when she told me again she had been kidnapped. So I said, 'Why haven't you done anything to find her?' Then she'd just shut down again."

That same conversation would play out again and again over the years, until 2014, when they had their last conversation.

"I don't want to talk to her," says Allison. "She doesn't want to give me any answers. I can't see, as a mother, how you can walk away. Anytime anybody tried to offer her assistance—uncles, grandparents, even social services—she said, "No, leave it alone. It's none of their business." There's a secret there, and I think it's that she knew Floyd had her the day Suzy was gone."

Chapter 13

Megan

The headstone at the Park Grove Cemetery in Broken Arrow, Oklahoma, bore a single name, that of a young woman who had spent only eight months in Oklahoma, where, before she was murdered, her daily routine was dancing at a sleazy strip club in nearby Tulsa.

Actually, "sleazy" is perhaps a bit too kind in describing Passions. The place was a rat hole that attracted an equally lowbrow crowd. In another world it would have been the last place that a brilliant high school student with dreams of working on the space shuttle could be found. But there she was, dancing and stripping seven days a week without rest, and at the end of each long night handing over all of her cash to the man she once called father, who now was her husband.

Unbeknownst to the few girls she had befriended at Passions, her name "Tonya" was stolen from a headstone in Alabama during a hurried escape from Florida after her murderous husband brutally tortured and shot to death a teenager, Cheryl Commesso.

But "Tonya" was the name they knew her by, and it would be the name they inscribed on the marker that rested on her grave at the Park Grove Cemetery.

It was a noble effort by several young women whose own difficult lives led them to the same dump of a strip club in the middle of the country. But beyond their own quiet misery and host of problems, the hearts of these hardened women had been touched by "Tonya." And despite the wishes of her husband to immediately cremate his wife's remains, they stepped in to ensure that she had a dignified burial.

So years later, while I was visiting the gravesite in 2003, I had a hope that one day the name on that headstone could be changed. It was a big wish, and as the years went by I thought it would remain just that. But thanks to Ashley Rodriguez at the National Center for Missing & Exploited Children and FBI agents Scott Lobb and Nate Furr, the time had come to make that wish come true. So my first call in October 2016 went to Megan Dufresne.

Megan was the baby girl given up for adoption in New Orleans by Tonya and Clarence Hughes in August 1989.

I first learned about Megan in 2005 from her mother, Mary, and I would speak to her soon after. She was bright, inquisitive, and, from what Mary told me, a brilliant student, much like her biological mother. Over the years we would speak from time to time and she would have questions about the book. For instance, in 2011, already aware of Michael, she wanted to know if there was news regarding Sharon's first child, a boy who, Sharon told her friend Jennifer Fisher, had been adopted. An only child, Megan wanted to find her biological brothers, but there wasn't much I could do.

I did watch from afar as Megan graduated from high school, then college in May of 2012 (cum laude), and then received her master's degree.

On October 2, 2014, Mary and Megan were the first people I contacted after learning from Joe Fitzpatrick that Sharon's true identity had been discovered. My message to them was as simple as Fitzpatrick's: call me.

Mary was shaken and happy when I delivered the news. She knew it was something Megan had wanted to hear. I would spend the next two days reaching out to members of Megan's newfound biological family. First up was her uncle Jim Chipman. He was a long haul trucker who lived in Michigan with his wife, Cindy. He filled me in on his sister Sandra, her then husband, Cliff Sevakis, and the ensuing years after Suzanne disappeared. Jim didn't have much to say about Sandra other than that she was a troubled woman he didn't have much of a relationship with. There was also his anger towards her over the disappearance of Suzanne. Jim loved the little girl, and after she went missing he had tried with his father to search for her. But with little information, and even less cooperation from his sister, their efforts proved fruitless. I told Jim that his niece had a grown daughter, and I sent Mary and Megan his phone number.

I also found Sandra. I was expecting to speak to a woman overcome with emotion and gratitude (toward the FBI and National Center) over the discovery of the fate of her oldest daughter. Instead, the conversation was cold. I didn't know her full story yet, but from what Sandra told me it wasn't pretty. (I would later learn of multiple children from different fathers, a lot of moving, little money, and no hint of regret over the fate of her oldest daughter. It became obvious to me that Megan should take careful steps connecting to this side of her biological family).

That said, I told Sandra she had a granddaughter and asked if she was interested in speaking to her. She said yes, so I emailed Sandra's contact information to Mary and Megan and left it up to them.

Originally excited and overwhelmed at the prospect of speaking with and meeting her biological grandmother, Megan would eventually speak with Sandra, but there would be no happy ending here. Despite a promising first call, Sandra's interest in Megan faded over time, and Mary and Megan canceled a trip in 2015 to meet in Virginia. It just didn't feel right, they said, and there were mushrooming questions about Sandra's culpability in Sharon's disappearance with Floyd. Mary and her husband Dean had raised Megan in a loving and nourishing home, and it became clear to them that it was in Megan's best interest not to engage with Sandra.

Unfortunately, I had the same concerns, so in the fall of 2016 it was Megan I called about replacing the headstone in Broken Arrow, Oklahoma. It was one thing for me to want to do it, but it was important to have a family member on board. And Megan was the obvious choice. We had finally met in person earlier that year. Megan and Mary were being interviewed in March for an Investigation Discovery channel/ABC News program, *20/20 on ID*, which would tell the Sharon Marshall story. I had known the producer, Peter Bull, for years. We met when we first began covering the Robert Durst story in the early 2000s. He was at ABC News then and I was reporting on Durst for *People* magazine and *Reader's Digest*. He was now at Lincoln Square Productions, an ABC News affiliate, and with the revelation of Sharon's true identity he wanted to tell her story. We had always wanted to work together and, with the book as the guide, I agreed to participate. He flew me down to New Orleans to meet the Dufresnes. When I arrived at Mary's house, she gave me a big hug, as if we had known each other for years (we actually had), and then she introduced me to Megan. It was an introduction I had looked forward to for a very long time.

Mary had cooked some of her New Orleans specialties while Peter and his film crew were taping everything, including the arrival of Jennifer Fisher. Jenny had also connected with Mary and Megan, and she cried when she met and embraced her best friend's daughter. It was remarkable to see all this happening.

I quietly told Megan that weekend about my plans to replace the headstone, and she was all for it. But there were some hurdles, chiefly getting permission from the cemetery to change the stone. I had called and explained the situation to the director there, who told me that only the person whose name was on the deed could make any changes. That meant I had to find that person and get written permission from him or her. I learned it was the wife of the club owner, J.R. Buck, whose name was on the deed. But I was told that she had died and that Buck was in ill health. So after a series of phone calls and Facebook messages, I found Buck's half-brother, who said he'd get in touch with Buck's daughter. Several months would pass without a word, and I eventually reached out to Mark Yancey and Ed Kumiega in Oklahoma City.

Mark was now the acting U.S. Attorney for the Western District of Oklahoma, and Ed was still an assistant U.S. attorney there. Since meeting them in 2003 I had remained in touch with both. I told them about the difficulties I was having getting permission to change the headstone, and both said they'd step in and take care of any of the legal work. Fortunately, I did finally connect with Buck's daughter, and she OK'd the change.

It was now early April 2017, and our plan was to make the change sometime during the summer. But Megan had some news. She was pregnant. The baby was due in August, and there was more. She was going to have a son and would name him Michael, in tribute to her half-brother, who had been missing since 1994. Megan wanted to keep her pregnancy a secret and also wanted to have the headstone ceremony in early June. She said her pregnancy would be somewhat difficult, and she was under doctor's orders to refrain from traveling after mid-June.

We picked Saturday, June 3. I called the cemetery and the director recommended two local monument shops. I called one, Gifford Monuments, and spoke to a fellow named Keith Millis. I explained what I was doing, and he was more than helpful. In fact, he was intrigued with the backstory and asked if I could send him a copy of *A Beautiful Child*, which I did. He called me back a few days later and said he had read the book. He also said that he had just retired as pastor for the Broken Arrow Police Department and asked if he could deliver Sharon's eulogy. He said it would be an honor. Of course I said yes.

I then emailed Merle Bean, Jennifer Fisher, Lynn Clemons, Karen Parsley, Jim and Cindy Chipman, and FBI agents Scott Lobb and Nate Furr. All but Furr said they would be there. (Furr was on assignment.) I also reached out to Joe Fitzpatrick, Mark Yancey, and Ed Kumiega. They not only said they would be there, but they wanted to contribute to the cost of the headstone. I told them it wasn't necessary, but they insisted. Despite the thousands of criminal cases each of them had worked over their careers, Sharon's story remained dear to them.

So we had a date, June 3, and a hotel, a newly opened La Quinta in Broken Arrow where those of us coming from out of town would meet and stay. But this plan to say good-bye to Sharon would take yet another turn when we added a name to the small, private list of attendees, Cliff Sevakis.

Chapter 14:
Cliff

I t was around 11:00 p.m. on April 15, 2017, when my cell phone pinged. I usually shut the sound off before going to bed, but for some reason on this night I didn't and my phone let me know I had a new email. I reached over and grabbed it from the nightstand and was stunned to see whom it was from: It was Cliff Sevakis.

I had reached out to Cliff more than two years earlier, on October 14, 2014, after I first learned Sharon's true identity. I searched for and found an email address, and sent him a brief message: Could we talk about your daughter Suzanne?

His response then was short and terse: "I have nothing to say, now or in the future."

Before that day, I had never heard of Cliff Sevakis. All I could put together was that he lived near Seattle and had a website, which is how I found him.

I did learn a little more from his former brother-in-law Jim Chipman, but not nearly enough to include in my blog post, "Finally," in which I reported October 4, 2014 the slimmest of details that the FBI had solved the mystery of Sharon's identity. Until that day, Cliff had never existed.

That changed two and a half years later. Cliff was ready to tell his story.

Mr. Birkbeck:

I guess that now, two years after learning the horrific fate of my daughter, Suzanne, I feel I am ready to speak with you about it. I did note that you were careful in assigning blame to Suzanne's parents and I am grateful that you did not choose to sensationalize and further victimize my ex-wife and I. There is enough guilt and suffering to go around.

I should tell you that I have been in contact with Mary Dufresne in New Orleans and had a promising conversation with my granddaughter, Megan. She seems to be a very good person and I am pleased to begin a relationship with her. At least one positive thing can come from all this sorrow.

I have told my wife that I may get past the heart-rending sadness that came with the knowledge your book brought me, but I will never get over it. After two years filled with many sleepless nights and sessions with my minister, prayer group and psychologist, I have begun to own up to this dark chapter in our lives. I look forward to talking with you and I thank you for your work in drawing attention to these unforgiveable crimes against so many child victims.

Sincerely,
Cliff Sevakis

It was perhaps the most honest and emotional letter I ever read, and I responded the next morning, telling him I understood his pain and asked if we could chat on the phone. We spoke a few days later. You could tell this was a man struggling with deep despair.

He told me he last saw his daughter in the early 1970s, that it was hard for him to acknowledge that, but there was a story behind it and he wanted to set the record straight, for good or bad.

His story began in June of 2014. Cliff was living in a Detroit suburb and had retired from a marketing career that included work for Ford. He had remarried when he was twenty-eight, had two children, and had studied for his master's degree.

He and his wife had just sold their home and were in the process of packing boxes for a move to Seattle to be near their two children, he said, when the doorbell rang. His wife answered and he was summoned into the living room, where he was introduced to two FBI agents and a Michigan state trooper.

"What's this about?" he asked.

The taller agent, Scott Lobb, asked Cliff to sit down, and he didn't mince words, asking if he had had a child long ago.

Cliff was caught off guard, and he paused. He was asked a question about a subject he hadn't discussed in years. Lobb didn't wait for a reply. He said he knew that Cliff had a daughter in 1969, that the mother's name was Sandra, that Cliff had been briefly married to her, and that the relationship ended in divorce.

"Yes, I did have a daughter," Cliff replied. "Her name was Suzanne."

Then, in detail, he told the story of how he had married his high school sweetheart, was drafted into the army, and learned she was pregnant just before he got shipped off to Vietnam.

He said he first saw Suzanne during a family visit in Hawaii when she was just a few months old. She was beautiful, with golden hair and a smile a mile wide. But his relationship with Sandra had clearly changed. She wanted a divorce, but agreed to reconsider and wait until Cliff returned home.

Cliff was young and his immediate goal was surviving his tour in Southeast Asia, after which he planned to return to Michigan and repair his relationship with his equally young wife. It wasn't long after Sandra returned home that he received a letter from his father Ray telling him that she was leaving him for another man.

Cliff returned home on a three-week leave and saw and played with his daughter. On his final day he again asked Sandra to reconsider, but this time she said no. She was seeing a man, Dennis Brandenburg, and she wanted to marry him. Cliff filed for divorce, but Michigan law required a one-year reconciliation period. By September 1970, he learned from his father that Sandra was pregnant and she was due to give birth in October. On September 14, 1970, Ray wrote to his son's attorney informing him that Sandra was pregnant with another man's baby and that she was due to give birth in another month or so. Cliff showed the FBI agents a copy of the letter:

I am writing to you to advise of developments that could have a bearing on the divorce action you are handling for my son, Clifford R. Sevakis. My daughter-in-law Sandi is expecting the child of Dennis Brandenburg about the end of October. I spoke to Dennis and Sandi today. They are anxious to marry prior to the time of their child's birth. It seems to me that there are sufficient reasons here to petition the court for an early action on the divorce petition. For instance, consider the stigma placed upon the innocent, unborn child of carrying a name other than that of its natural father; also the possibility that the court would place upon Clifford the burden of supporting a child not his and symbolic of a great sorrow and failure in his life.

Mr. Brandenburg indicated to me that he would be willing to commit to writing his intent to marry Sandi when the law allows.

They do not have a telephone. Sandi tells me that their mail delivery is very slow and at times rather uncertain. Should it become necessary to communicate with them hurriedly, I would be willing to serve as a courier. In view of the reputed glacial speed of the courts as opposed to the imminence of Sandi's delivery, some quick action is indicated, if, in your opinion, the suggested action is feasible.

Allison Sevakis was born on October 19, 1970, and Cliff was listed on her birth certificate as her father. He was discharged from the army in 1971, but by then Sandra had moved to North Carolina. In 1972, Cliff decided to drive there with a friend to visit Suzanne. He stayed in a motel, where he played his acoustic guitar for Suzanne and Allison. He also bought the girls crayons. Suzanne wouldn't let go of her Snow White coloring book. It was the last time Cliff would ever see her.

Two years later, on June 17, 1974, he received a call from the Gastonia County, North Carolina, Department of Social Services. Suzanne, Allison, and another child, Amy, had been taken away from Sandra and were now in state custody. The caseworker asked if Cliff would be willing to either take all three children, or give up his parental rights to Suzanne and Allison so they could be adopted by the same family.

Cliff had been working as a disc jockey at a local radio station but made next to nothing and, at twenty-four, he considered himself "messed up" and not ready for civilization. Still, he said he might consider caring for his own daughter. But the social worker said the three little girls were very close, and Cliff didn't want to separate them. So he agreed to give up his parental rights to Suzanne and Allison, who legally remained his daughter though, he had been told, she was Dennis Brandenburg's child. He signed the Parent's Release, Surrender, and Consent to Adoption form, had them notarized, and mailed them back.

But just a week later, on June 28, 1974, he received another letter from Gastonia County. It appeared that Sandra's situation had changed dramatically.

Dear Mr. Sevakis,

We are in receipt of the Release for Adoption forms relative to Suzanne and Allison, forms which you signed on 6-21-74.

We are writing at this point to inform you of recent happenings in the situation of your former wife, Sandra C. Brandenburg Williams. She is now remarried and on 6-19-74 requested that her consent to adoption for these two children be revoked and, as a result of this and other circumstances, we had no alternative but to return the children to Mrs. Williams, such placement occurring on 6-21-74.

As far as we can ascertain, the forms you signed relative to release are still valid unless revoked within thirty days of your signing.

We have advised your former wife and her attorney that these consents have been given.

We appreciate your concern and cooperation in this matter.

Cliff said that was the last time he ever heard about Sandra or Suzanne.

The other agent, Nate Furr, pulled out several photos of a young girl and asked Cliff if he recognized her.

"Can that be your daughter?" said Furr.

Maybe, Cliff replied.

He listened intently as Lobb and Furr told the story about a young woman named Tonya Hughes who was killed in Oklahoma City in 1990. She had a little boy, Michael, they said, who was later kidnapped from his school and was never seen again.

"The girl had lived with a man, Franklin Floyd, and they had shown up in Oklahoma City in 1975 when she was a little girl. Her name was Suzanne Davis," Cliff recalled Furr telling him.

Cliff tried his best to make sense of what he was hearing. But then came the sudden realization that something awful had occurred, and the anguish overwhelmed him.

"That's my daughter?"

"We believe so," said Lobb.

Cliff was shattered. The two agents could see his emotions were real and they were sympathetic towards him after having dredged up his distant, painful past.

"We'd like to take a swab from you for a DNA test to confirm she is your daughter Suzanne," said Lobb.

Sickened by the story he had just heard, Cliff agreed.

The agents and the troopers left, leaving Cliff behind to ponder what if. A few weeks later, he received the call that the DNA test, matched against the blood that Megan had provided some years earlier, was positive.

Sharon Marshall was Suzanne Marie Sevakis.

It took Cliff nearly three years to come to terms with the decisions he had made so long ago, some of which he believed had contributed to Suzanne's horrific life and death. His email to me was heartfelt. I told him about our plan to replace his daughter's gravestone and invited him to come. He immediately said yes.

Chapter 15:

Saying Good-bye

O n Thursday, June 1, 2017, I boarded a plane in Newark, New Jersey, and flew out to Tulsa, Oklahoma, to do something that, frankly, I never thought would happen: replace Sharon's gravestone.

I'd been back to Oklahoma the previous summer to interview Scott Lobb and Nate Furr in Oklahoma City, but this was my first trip back to Tulsa since 2003. It was early evening when my flight arrived at Tulsa airport, and I drove straight to the La Quinta Inn in nearby Broken Arrow. The hotel was new, its grand-opening banners still hanging across the front, and it would serve as the temporary home for those of us traveling from other parts of the U.S. Lynn Clemons (who changed his last name to Thornton) was already there, having arrived that afternoon from New Orleans. Jim and Cindy Chipman would drive in the next day from Michigan, while Mary and Dean Defense and a pregnant Megan all flew up from New Orleans that Friday afternoon. Cliff Sevakis checked in on Friday night after a long flight from Seattle, while Jennifer Fisher had perhaps the most arduous journey, having begun her drive from Florida a couple of days earlier.

I had some things to do that Friday morning, the first of which was to drive over to Park Grove Cemetery. The new headstone had been set the day before and I wanted to get a look before everyone else. Keith Millis had become my guiding hand here, having overseen the preparation of the stone, from its markings to its setting. But of course I was still a bit nervous and wanted to make sure there were no issues with the name, such as a misspelling or factual error. (I had worked for a newspaper early in my career that printed a story saying the Japanese attack on Pearl Harbor occurred in November 1942. So, yes, I try to be careful).

Park Grove is not a big cemetery. It sits between two residential developments off West Houston Street, a major thoroughfare. Once you drive in and onto the narrow inner road, you pass the main office on the right and then make the first left, go down a bit, and then the first right. Sharon's grave sits in the back, just off the road, on the right and under an oak tree.

As I pulled up I could see the new headstone had been set. A piece of blue carpeting covered the face and back and was partially covered by green garbage bags that were duct taped to its base. It was kind of flimsy, but when I slowly pulled the carpeting away and saw the new marker, I was floored. It said SEVAKIS and then, underneath, SUZANNE MARIE. Below was her birthdate, SEPT. 6, 1969, and underneath that APRIL 30, 1990, the day she died. Scrolled across the bottom was DEVOTED MOTHER AND FRIEND. Megan and I had thought long and hard about what should be written there. Actually, it was really Megan's decision. We initially sought opinions from several others, but in the end there were too many voices with too many ideas, and the main aim was to keep it simple yet dignified. Megan was the daughter, and I was there to help. We agreed we weren't going to place any of the stolen names and aliases she had used during her life, not even Sharon. Only one name mattered, her real one.

Once that was settled we turned to what would go underneath the name. One suggestion was "Mother to Michael and Megan," but that wasn't going to work. Megan considered Mary her mother and didn't want to disrespect her in any way. So after some discussion we came up with "Devoted Mother and Friend." It spoke the truth of Sharon's life. She loved her son, Michael, so much that she died trying to save him from Floyd. And she loved her friends, Jennifer Fisher and Lynn Clemons, who both went on to graduate from college and to successful careers, spurred in part by her encouragement.

Elsewhere, silhouettes of roses were carved into the left and right upper corners, and in the center, above the name, was something that caused my eyes to open wide: a picture of Suzanne.

Pastor Keith Millis had asked a few weeks earlier if he could place a silhouette of her on the stone. He said everyone at Gifford Memorial felt so strongly about what we were doing they wanted to add it at no charge. But this was something more. It was her high school graduation photo, in color and imprinted on marble and attached to the stone. It was beautiful.

I stood there for a few minutes admiring Keith's work, and I couldn't help but think that yet another person had been touched by Sharon's story. As it turned out, I had to leave to meet with Keith. We had scheduled lunch at his favorite restaurant, the Apple Barrel Café. He had suggested the restaurant after I told him we were looking for a place to eat after the ceremony, but he wanted me to see it first. To that point we had only spoken over the phone, but as soon as I arrived I could hear a soft yet distinct Oklahoma accent calling to me, and I knew it was him.

Keith was close to eighty years old and walked with the aid of a cane due to some issues with his feet. After we sat down he said he had spent several days working on the eulogy. As Broken Arrow's police pastor for many years, he was accustomed to this. But the pastor said he wanted it to be perfect, and he appeared to be perhaps a bit nervous. I had no idea what to expect from him other than to believe he'd say a few meaningful words. After our lunch, I headed over to the florist Keith knew in downtown Broken Arrow. The idea was to have a wreath above the stone and then flowers on the side. In addition, I ordered three dozen red roses that we would hand out after the eulogy. I'm typically not the guy doing the planning and picking out roses, etc. But here I was, commiserating with the florist, making sure everything would be perfect for the pickup the next morning. It was a bit surreal.

When I returned to the hotel that afternoon, some of the other people had arrived. Jim and Cindy Chipman had made the long drive from Michigan, and our introduction was warm. Then came Mary, Dean and Megan Dufresne. Jim was the only biological family member there who actually knew and remembered Suzanne and his introduction to Megan was emotional. Lynn Clemons would join the conversation, and we all spent the rest of the afternoon at the small hotel bar talking. It was around 6:30 p.m. when Cliff Sevakis texted me. His flight had just arrived and he was getting into his rental car. I told him we had made dinner reservations and, yes, he said he would join us. A few minutes later, Cliff arrived. He was of medium height and looked younger than his sixty-five years. He embraced Jim Chipman, whom he hadn't seen in years. And then he saw Megan.

Cliff is somewhat reserved, as is Megan. To say this moment was awkward would be kind. Since first speaking in April they had had several phone conversations, but now Cliff was face-to-face with the granddaughter whom, for most of her life, he had not even known existed. It had to be terribly difficult for them to meet under these circumstances, but they both smiled and hugged.

Watching was Mary, who looked like she was floating on a cloud. Mary is one of those people whose good humor and positive vibes just flow from her being, and she was truly happy that Megan had finally met members of her biological family. Mary's secret hope was that the connection would last.

Jennifer Fisher was still on the road and not due to arrive for a few more hours, but the rest of us headed for the restaurant, where we ate, drank, talked, and laughed. Everyone was getting to know each other, and the goodwill would flow through to the next morning of what would be a day to remember.

The wreath of yellow, pink, and purple roses was placed behind the new headstone, while sunflowers were placed on each side.

The sunny weather the day before gave way to a gray, cool, misty morning, and a light rain began to fall. It was around 10:00 a.m., and I had picked up the flowers before driving over to the cemetery. We had planned to begin at 11:00 a.m., then have the unveiling and ceremony. Finally, everyone would head to the Apple Barrel for lunch.

I was tending to the flowers when a local TV news crew pulled up. One of the TV stations wanted to visit us the day before for their evening news, but that wasn't a good idea given that we wanted a semiprivate ceremony. So we asked them to wait until the following morning, and they agreed. A few minutes later Pastor Keith arrived. He pulled out a red-striped blanket emblazoned with the blue Broken Arrow, Oklahoma, police insignia and suggested placing it over the new stone until he finished his eulogy, at which point we'd make the big reveal and hand out the roses. It was a little theatrical but it sounded like a good idea. So we covered the stone with the blanket as the first cars entered the cemetery and slowly snaked through the narrow road towards us.

Tulsa is a two-hour drive from Oklahoma City, yet among the first to arrive were the law enforcement officials who played such a vital role in this story, most of them faces I hadn't seen since 2003. Mark Yancey and Ed Kumiega drove up separately with their wives. Eddie and I had been in regular contact over the years, usually trading phone calls. I was glad to see them both. Soon after, I spotted Joe Fitzpatrick walking towards us. It was good to see Joe, who had spent so much time, before and after his retirement, on this case. And then there were Merle and Ernest Bean, who had driven up from the same home in Choctaw where they raised Michael before his kidnapping. Karen Parsley, Sharon's friend from the Passions club, was there, as was Jennifer Fisher, who had finally made it to town late the night before. I had seen Jenny the previous year in New Orleans for the taping of the *20/20* program, but she hadn't seen Yancey, Kumiega, or Fitzpatrick since 1995, when they brought her to Oklahoma City to testify in Floyd's kidnapping trial.

And then there was FBI agent Scott Lobb, who also had driven up from Oklahoma City. His work with Nate Furr interrogating Floyd should become a required class at the FBI training facility in Quantico, Virginia.

All these people were coming together, some from great distances, and they huddled in small circles introducing themselves to each other. Those who were already familiar with each other reacted with warm embraces, among them Jenny Fisher, who hugged Yancey and Kumiega and practically everyone else.

By 11:00 a.m. everyone had arrived, and it was a few minutes later when Pastor Keith asked all to come forward around the grave. The light rain had stopped, the birds were chirping, and with his back resting against the front of his car (to relieve the pain in his bad feet), he began by commenting on how the young woman buried there must have been very special for all of us to have come.

"Matt asked me if I could share this with you today, and I said this would be an honor. I read his book twice and feel like a lot of you. I don't know your faces, but I know what you've been through. The one thing that stuck out in my mind is that Sharon—I know it was *Suzanne*, but so many times in reading through there her most popular name was Sharon, so excuse me if I use that name—but she touched so many lives."

Keith spoke for about fifteen minutes, intermixing scripture with his observations on how despite her "tremendous ordeal ... Sharon touched our lives during her short twenty years." True to his promise, Keith didn't take this lightly. He spoke to Sharon's friendships, her love for Michael, and the dedication of people like Joe Fitzpatrick, a hardened investigator who had solved every case with the exception of one prior to his retirement.

"I think of Joe and the tenacity that this man had. I think of the years you literally spent on this case," said Keith, looking at the FBI veteran. "One of the things I read was how Joe didn't have a case he didn't finish. The thing going on with Joe was the tenacity ... law enforcement is not a job; it's a calling. I mean that, Joe. I sense that she touched your life and it became a very dedicated opportunity and task of finding out everything that you could ... I think of all the FBI people and the detectives down in Florida. You were all affected by her life."

Standing in the back, I scanned the small gathering of thirty or so people and saw a father who hadn't seen his daughter in forty-five years getting to see her last resting place; a daughter who was finally near her biological mother; and friends such as Lynn Clemons and Jennifer Fisher who were nurtured and cherished and had gotten the opportunity at last to say good-bye. This felt pretty good.

Keith ended his eulogy by quoting a scene from the book, the one in which Karen Parsley and another former dancer, LaVernia Watkins, visited Sharon's grave in 2003 following Floyd's conviction for murdering Cheryl Commesso.

"Karen said, 'I hope one day we find out who you really were. I hope one day I'll know your real name, and I'll meet your real family, and I can tell them I once knew a girl who tried to save herself and her son. And I can tell them I was your friend.' "

Keith asked me to take the blanket off the headstone. Everyone sort of froze as I handed out the roses. You could hear sobbing amidst the chirping from the birds, but then something happened. Mary wanted to say a few words. She was caught up in the moment, and her emotions took over as she spoke about how proud she was of Megan, how great it was to meet Cliff, and how this morning had so much meaning. Then Cliff raised his hand and walked to the center of our group.

"I am Suzanne's biological father," he said. "You know, many times none of us would choose a particular path in life that was mine, but the amazing thing about my daughter, who I last saw when she was three years old, was that she did so much good in the short time she was here. She was such a beautiful person that we're all here today because just not her beauty but her beautiful soul. For all of you who've done so much in her memory, I just want to say thanks."

There was a pause for a few seconds when another, quieter voice called out from the side. It was Merle Bean. With her husband Ernest's arm around her back, she spoke about Michael and what it meant for them to be there that day. The Beans were simple people who tried to do good for so many foster children and it seemed unfair, even diabolical, that someone like a Franklin Floyd could have affected their lives in such a horrible way. But they never mentioned his name. No one did. Not Cindy Chipman, Lynn Clemons, or Joe Fitzpatrick. And especially not Megan. Eight months pregnant with a boy she would name Michael and teary-eyed, she moved to the center holding a single rose with both hands.

"Being in my position, I wouldn't know any of this if is wasn't for the work you all done here," she said as her voiced choked with emotion. "I've been blessed with where I am because Lord knows where I would be otherwise. I have so many new relationships and more family than I need, and I hope I can be half the mom that she was."

With that, Keith took the police blanket that had covered the headstone and placed it around Megan's shoulders.

"That's for you," he whispered.

Amidst the tears and some clapping, Lynn Clemons approached the headstone and laid down his rose at the base. The idea had been for all the mourners to take their roses with them, but one by one they followed Lynn's lead, and soon the grave was covered in red roses.

It was an organic moment, and it was a beautiful end to an emotional morning. I had worried how this would turn out, but frankly the spirit of the morning took over and it was a hundred times better than I ever imagined.

The ceremony was over, and we'd all eventually head over to the Apple Barrel. But lunch would wait a while. People lingered, not wanting to say good-bye just yet. Some knelt in front of the grave; others just stood with their heads bowed.

Cliff Sevakis would come back that afternoon, alone, and he'd spend some time quietly talking to the daughter he really never knew.

Whether he sought forgiveness or absolution or just wanted to say how sorry he was, I don't really know. He and I had dinner together that night and I didn't want to ask. Cliff was at peace, and whatever he said was between him and his daughter.

Suzanne Marie Sevakis.

Epilogue

Megan Dufresne gave birth to her son Michael on July 16, 2017. She remained in touch with her grandfather Cliff Sevakis, who sent her gifts welcoming his great-grandson. She also received gifts from her uncle Jim Chipman and his wife, Cindy. And they all exchanged cards and gifts for Christmas.

But the story still wasn't over.

On March 7, 2019, I received a message via Facebook.

Hello, I have a question for you. I think I may have been in one of your books. My dad died last Sunday and my adopted mother told me my real last name last night. This all sounds strange. I just need some answers and I think you may be able to help me.

It was from a Steve Patterson, and he said he believed he was the long, lost baby Philip, the infant boy given up by Sandra back in 1974 after she had met Franklyn Floyd.

After hearing from Steve, I told him we could try a DNA test and I reached out to Scott Lobb in Oklahoma City. I told him about Steve's message and asked if he could facilitate the test. Lobb never bought into the story of the missing infant, but to his credit he said sure. It would take months to get a result, so during that time I learned a little bit more from Steve.

He said he was born, raised and still lived in North Carolina. His father after his father died his mother, Mary, took him aside to show him some documents. His real name, she told him, was Philip Brandenburg.

Mary explained that she once knew Sandi Brandenburg. They had lived near each other in Gaston County and they had been in the hospital together. Mary had just lost another pregnancy and was distraught, while Sandi, who couldn't care for the three daughters she already had, was pregnant again a fourth child. Several weeks had passed when Sandi knocked on Mary's door. She explained that she was leaving town with her new husband and three daughters but she couldn't take care of an infant. Mary recalls seeing Floyd off in the distance watching as Sandi gave Philip to Mary and left town, never to be seen again.

Mary changed his name to Steven and she raised him with her husband as their own. Steve said he's had a good life, and still does, but it was turned upside down after his father died. He said he needed to know for sure if he was, in fact, Sandi's biological son.

It would take nearly a year but in February 2020 Steve called me to say the DNA result was in: He was indeed Sandi's son, and Suzanne's little brother.

I met Steve in Virginia in March 2021 while filming the Netflix documentary *Girl in the Picture*, which was based on "A Beautiful Child" and this book. I liked Steve a lot. Quiet spoken and down to earth, he was still trying to process the entire story. By then he had already connected with Jim Chipman, Sandra's brother, and was planning to travel to Florida to visit Jim and Jim's father – Steve's grandfather – Chip Chipman.

Steve has also reached out to Suzanne's biological daughter Megan – his niece – and her mother Mary and they remain in contact.

Connecting different family members who didn't know they existed has been among the most rewarding parts of this story. Aside from Steve forging new relationships with the Chipman's, Megan remains close with her grandfather Cliff Sevakis and his wife Jen, who flew in from the west coast to attend her wedding in November 2021 to her long-time love Jacob Dufreche. It was quite a sight to see Cliff and Megan dance together, much like it was to see the photo of a smiling Steve hanging with his uncle and grandfather.

Connecting different family members who didn't know they even existed has been among the most rewarding parts of this story. And I like to think that when all is said and done, despite the horror and evil of Franklin Floyd, it was the humanity of a young woman who most of us had never known that made it possible, and finally gave us the hopeful end to a terrible story.

Steve Patterson with his newfound family in Florida, March 2021. Steve (center) with uncle Jim Chipman (right) and grandfather Chip Chipman (left).

Megan and Cliff at Megan's wedding, November 2021.

HEADSTONE CEREMONY, JUNE 3, 2017

Sharon's old headstone with the name Tonya at the Park Grove Cemetery in Broken Arrow, Oklahoma. It took over twenty-five years, but a new marker with her real name was unveiled before old friends, family and law enforcement in June 2017.

Acting U.S. Attorney Mark Yancey greeting Jennifer Fisher (above) at the gravestone ceremony, June 2017 (as Lynn Clemons looks on). They last saw each other during Franklin Floyd's kidnapping trial in 1995.

Assistant U.S. Attorney Ed Kumiega meeting Cliff Sevakis.

Michael's foster parents Ernest and Merle Bean.
(Photo courtesy of Matt Birkbeck).

Joe Fitzpatrick (talking with Jennifer Fisher). The retired FBI agent flew to Washington, D.C. at the request of the National Center in 2012 to help with their efforts to identify Sharon Marshall.
(Photo courtesy of Matt Birkbeck)

Former Broken Arrow police pastor Keith Millis. Nearing 80,
he delivered a poignant, heartfelt eulogy. He passed away in 2022.
(Photo courtesy of Matt Birkbeck).

Pastor Millis draped the police blanket that covered Suzanne's grave over Megan.
(Photo courtesy of Matt Birkbeck).

Jim and Cindy Chipman. Jim and his father tried to find Suzanne
after she disappeared in 1975, but his sister Sandra didn't give them much to go on.
Cindy told of his heartbreak following the ceremony.
(Photo courtesy of Matt Birkbeck).

Mary Dufresne (center). She met "Clarence and Tonya Hughes" in 1989,
and adopted the infant daughter she'd name Megan.
(Photo courtesy of Mary Dufresne).

Jennifer Fisher and "Ray Baby" Lynn (Thornton) Clemons.
(Photo courtesy of Mary Dufresne).

Cliff Sevakis laying down a rose at his daughter's grave. He last saw Suzanne in 1972.
(Photo courtesy of Matt Birkbeck).

A terrible story begins a meaningful new chapter as a grandfather meets his granddaughter.
(Photo courtesy of Matt Birkbeck).

Acknowledgments

This was a short book that took a long time to come together, and it wouldn't have without the help of several people.

FBI agent Terry Weber, who helped facilitate the interviews with Scott Lobb and Nate Furr in June 2016 in Oklahoma City; Scott Lobb and Nate Furr, for giving me their time then, and after; Ashley Rodriguez of the National Center for Missing & Exploited Children; FBI agent Joe Fitzpatrick (retired); Former U.S. Attorney in Oklahoma Mark Yancey and AUSA Ed Kumiega; Keith Millis, pastor, Broken Arrow Police Department (retired); Peter Bull, television producer.

And special thanks to Don Armstrong, a real pro I've known for years for carefully editing this book.

About The Author

Matt Birkbeck is an award-winning investigating journalist, best-selling author, and the executive producer of the Netflix documentary *Girl in the Picture,* which is based on his books "A Beautiful Child and "Finding Sharon."

Books by Matt Birkbeck

A Deadly Secret (Berkley/Penguin 2002)

A Beautiful Child (Berkley/Penguin 2004)

Till Death Do Us Part (Atria/Simon & Schuster 2006)

Deconstructing Sammy (Amistad/Harper Collins 2008)

The Quiet Don (Berkley/Penguin 2013)

Finding Sharon (Summerville 2018)

The Life We Chose (William Morrow/Harper Collins 2023)

Selected postings from
MATT BIRKBECK'S BLOG

From his website www.mattbirkbeck.com

SHARON MARSHALL UPDATE
12/31/2010

I haven't had much to report over the last few months on the search for Sharon's identity. The trail had run cold with no new leads, until yesterday, when I spoke with Joe Stegall, a high school classmate of Sharon's at Forest Park. Joe reached out to me about a month ago, and we finally connected on the phone.

Joe had a crush on Sharon and relayed many of the similar experiences others described in their relationships with Sharon, especially her quick exit from phone calls whenever Floyd was around. But it was during those calls to Sharon's home that Joe said something interesting – he could hear a toddler in the background.

When Joe asked Sharon who it was she said it was her "little brother." According to Joe, the child was there in the house for some time, perhaps weeks, since he could hear him whenever he was on the phone with Sharon. I have no idea who the boy was or why he was in the home. It wasn't Michael, who was born two years later in 1988. Could the child have been another one of Floyd's victims and awaiting transfer or sale to someone else, much like Floyd sold Sharon's other children? I don't' know. It's just a guess.

Joe also mentioned that Sharon's son, Michael Anthony, was most likely named after Michael Anthony, the bassist in Sharon's favorite band, Van Halen.

LITTLE BROTHER OR ANOTHER VICTIM
1/25/2011

I spoke with one of the federal investigators who put Franklin Floyd in prison in 1995 (for kidnapping Michael Hughes) and passed along the tidbit from one of Sharon's classmates about hearing a toddler in the background during phone calls with Sharon.

His first thought was that perhaps it was Sharon's child. Then he thought again and suggested that the boy was another of Floyd's victims, stolen from his mother and headed for destination unknown.

There's really no way to know, but it does open a door into Floyd's world and prompts discussion as to whether he was even more of a monster than we believed.

As it stands he's still rotting in a Florida prison. Anyone hoping he'd get zapped into oblivion anytime soon will be disappointed to know some of the evidence from his trial was lost and he'll most likely avoid the executioner and live out the rest of his days on the taxpayers dime behind bars.

I've heard from a good number of readers who want to visit with Floyd hoping a passionate appeal would somehow lead him to divulging Sharon's origins. Forget it. You'd have better luck trying to talk a banana into peeling itself. I spent six hours with the man during prison interviews and came to the (quick) conclusion he was more than a sociopath – he was a vicious killer. That opinion was quickly formed after Floyd showed me disturbing photos he took of a severely beaten, nearly unconscious Cheryl Comes. He obtained the photos while representing himself during his murder trial, and they revealed how he had burned the young woman with cigarettes throughout her body. He also left her bloodied and near death before shooting her twice in the head.

We'll keep everyone posted when new leads come in.

TENNESSEE LINK

8/7/2013

It's been a year since I first mentioned a potential break in the search for Sharon's identity. Local and federal law enforcement have been involved, but to date there's been no significant movement or progress. So, here's what's been happening.

Police near Knoxville, TN received a call from a woman who said she knew Franklin Floyd when she was a child in the early 1970s, and that Floyd and his brother Billy had visited her father, who was a serial rapist and pedophile. Floyd was on the run (you'll recall he violated his parole in early 1973) and sought refuge with this woman's father. Around the same time, the body of Janet Carter was found in the Smokey Mountains and her three-year old daughter Christina was missing. Janet was from Birmingham and was in the midst of a custody battle with her husband when she fled. The woman claims that her father killed Janet and took Christina, whom he repeatedly raped before killing her and burying her body underneath his home.

Around the same time, Floyd and his brother were staying nearby, and the woman said she would be taken there every weekend, where Floyd would rape her. The woman remembers another little girl, a cousin, who was also repeatedly raped by her father. The cousin, said the woman, is Sharon.

The woman said her father was going to kill Sharon, but Floyd apparently fled with her.

The woman told her story to the local police, who called in the local FBI. Their interest was minimal. After six months, and with little progress, I connected the local police to Joe Fitzpatrick, and over the past few months the woman has been interviewed several times by an outside FBI bureau. There are other details that can't be released yet.

The woman says she never read A Beautiful Child, and her memories are real. I thought enough of her and her story to pass it along. The bit about Floyd "rescuing" the girl from the woman's father is similar to what Floyd told me when I interviewed him, that he saved the girl from certain death. The woman's father is still alive, and last I heard police were going to interview him. Will keep you posted.

MURDERS AND MOTIVES ON INVESTIGATION DISCOVERY CHANNEL

9/9/2014

From my book A Beautiful Child, the Investigation Discovery Channel is airing a program on Franklyn Floyd's murder of Cheryl Commesso with tie in to mystery of Sharon Marshall.

I interviewed a couple of months ago and looking forward to seeing the result. Program airs Sept. 29 at 8 pm ET.

FINALLY

10/3/2014

It's been ten years since the publication of A Beautiful Child and the one enduring question that had yet to be answered is "who was Sharon Marshall?"

There are thousands of readers around the world who've asked me that question, while many at organizations such as the Doe Network have tried to conduct their own searches. Readers sent names of missing children to me, and I forwarded them to either the National Center for Missing Children in D.C. or Joe Fitzpatrick, the retired FBI agent who lead the investigation into the Michael Hughes kidnapping. While we had Sharon's DNA sample, nothing matched.

On Wednesday, Oct. 1, I received a call from Joe informing me that Sharon had finally been positively identified. The details were sketchy, but he gave me the name. I then spoke to her family today (Friday). The news was true. I can't share all the details, but here's what I can say....

Her name is Suzanne Marie Savakis and she was from North Carolina.

For those who read the book, you'll recall Floyd fled Florida in 1973 after violating his parole. He ended up in North Carolina a year later using another alias and met a recently divorced woman with four children – three young daughters and infant son. Floyd and the woman later married, and in 1975 the woman was sentenced to 30 days in jail for a minor crime. When she was released Floyd was gone and so where her children. She found two daughters at a local social services agency, where Floyd had taken them. The mother went to the local police and FBI and tried to file kidnapping charges but they declined to investigate saying that since Floyd was their stepfather he apparently had a right to take the children.

Three months later, Floyd and Suzanne, then six years old, were in Oklahoma City. Her little brother was never found. The mother and her family, including her parents, brother and sister-in-law, never gave up the search. Alas, there wasn't much to go on.

Earlier this year the FBI interviewed Floyd in prison in Florida and somehow gleaned the info about the woman. They visited with her in June, showed her the photos of Floyd and Suzanne (her sitting on his lap). The woman immediately identified him as her husband and Sharon as her daughter. The agents took a DNA sample and four weeks later (in July) visited with the mother again to inform her the test was a positive match.

The young woman we knew as Sharon Marshall was indeed Suzanne.

The FBI then shared with her some details of Suzanne's sad fate, but recommended she read A Beautiful Child. The woman and her surviving children and family all read the book. Needless to say they are devastated. The agents also told the family not to discuss the case given they were also looking into the disappearance of Suzanne's son Michael.

Floyd apparently was also willing to give some information about Michael but sadly, he admitted to killing Michael and, I'm told, the FBI was resigned to believe him. The agents called the family this week with the news that Michael was likely dead. They have an idea of the location of his remains and plan to search the area.

Since the authorities in North Carolina didn't take a missing person report, Suzanne was never listed in any missing persons database, which is why it has been impossible to this point to find her. Suzanne's story was heartbreaking and, judging by reader responses, has touched them deeply, which is why many who have read the book and followed this case have kept it alive these years with their sleuthing, web postings and discussions. And that's why law enforcement remained involved for so long, with the incredible work of the FBI that brought it to a close. Others who had always been involved in the search include Gerry Nance of the NCMEC (since retired), Ed Kumiega, Asst. U.S. Attorney in

Oklahoma City, Bob Schock and Mark Deasaro of the St. Petersburg, Fla. Police Dept. and of course, Joe Fitzpatrick.

Joe retired from the FBI in the late 1990s but since our initial meeting fishing amidst the snakes in OKC in 2003, he and I have remained in steady contact. He funneled suggestions from readers to FBI officials, helped facilitate with Gerry Nance a number of DNA tests, and remained an integral part of the search for Sharon. There were some DNA tests where we had our hopes up, only to be eventually dashed. You'll recall Joe had resolved every one of his cases...except for one.

Now there are none.

In addition, our deep thanks and appreciation go to the FBI in Oklahoma City. There are other details I can't share yet but take my word they did amazing work.

Suzanne's family is still digesting all of this and will need some time. In addition, there may be a meeting with Suzanne's surviving daughter (whom you'll recall she gave birth to in New Orleans in 1989).

I'm in contact with the daughter, a beautiful college grad, who's expressed an interest in meeting her biological family. That may now happen sooner than later.

And finally, we can now put Suzanne's real name on her tombstone at the Park Grove Cemetery in Tulsa, Oklahoma.

Suzanne Marie Savakis.

Peace.

SAYING GOODBYE TO SHARON
10/29/2017

BROKEN ARROW – We said goodbye to Sharon Marshall in June. Her name here in Oklahoma had been "Tonya," and that was what was on her tombstone. But I always referred to her as Sharon. It was the name she had used during her high school years at Forest Park, Georgia in the 1980s when she was at her best. Of course, even that name was a fraud, stolen from somewhere like the other names she had been given by the man who had taken her as a child.

I first visited Broken Arrow, Oklahoma in 2003, and it was then when I saw the tombstone that said "Tonya." I had already spent nearly a year doing my research and interviews for what would become *A Beautiful Child*, and seeing the gravesite here in Broken Arrow with only a first name, and a stolen one at that, left me with a very unsettled feeling. By that time, having visited Florida and Georgia first, I knew Tonya as Sharon Marshall, and throughout the years that's what I always called her.

On June 3, we said goodbye to Sharon, and unveiled a new tombstone with her real name, Suzanne Sevakis. How that came about, the discovery of her real name, and the new friends and family found since the publication of *A Beautiful Child*, will be told as part of the new book, now scheduled for 2018. Will keep you posted.

Made in the USA
Monee, IL
20 February 2024

53847151R00104